OPPOSING VIEWPOINTS® SERIES

Politics and Journalism in a Post-Truth World

DISCARDED

Other Books of Related Interest

Opposing Viewpoints Series

The Fifth Estate: Extreme Viewpoints from Alternative Media
Identity Politics
Online Filter Bubbles

At Issue Series

Media Bias and the Role of the Press
Politicians on Social Media
Populism in the Digital Age

Current Controversies Series

Political Correctness
The Political Elite and Special Interests
Political Extremism in the United States

> "Congress shall make no law … abridging the freedom of speech, or of the press."

First Amendment to the US Constitution

The basic foundation of our democracy is the First Amendment guarantee of freedom of expression. The Opposing Viewpoints series is dedicated to the concept of this basic freedom and the idea that it is more important to practice it than to enshrine it.

OPPOSING
VIEWPOINTS®
SERIES

Politics and Journalism in a Post-Truth World

Martin Gitlin, Book Editor

GREENHAVEN
PUBLISHING

Published in 2019 by Greenhaven Publishing, LLC
353 3rd Avenue, Suite 255, New York, NY 10010

Copyright © 2019 by Greenhaven Publishing, LLC

First Edition

Articles in Greenhaven Publishing anthologies are often edited for length to meet page
requirements. In addition, original titles of these works are changed to clearly present
the main thesis and to explicitly indicate the author's opinion. Every effort is made to
ensure that Greenhaven Publishing accurately reflects the original intent of the authors.
Every effort has been made to trace the owners of the copyrighted material.

Cover image: wellphoto/Shutterstock.com

Library of Congress Cataloging-in-Publication Data

Names: Gitlin, Marty, editor.
Title: Politics and journalism in a post-truth world / Martin Gitlin, Book
  Editor.
Description: First edition. | New York : Greenhaven Publishing, 2019. |
  Series: Opposing viewpoints | Includes bibliographical references and
  index. | Audience: Grades 9–12.
Identifiers: LCCN 2018022313| ISBN 9781534504158 (library bound) | ISBN
  9781534504417 (pbk.)
Subjects: LCSH: Journalism—Political aspects—United States—History—21st
  century. | Journalism—Objectivity—United States. | Social
  media—Political aspects—United States. | United States—Politics and
  government—21st century—Press coverage. | Right and left (Political
  science)—United States.
Classification: LCC PN4751 .P613 2018 | DDC 070.4/49320973—dc23
LC record available at https://lccn.loc.gov/2018022313

Manufactured in the United States of America

Website: http://greenhavenpublishing.com

Contents

The Importance of Opposing Viewpoints

Perhaps every generation experiences a period in time in which the populace seems especially polarized, starkly divided on the important issues of the day and gravitating toward the far ends of the political spectrum and away from a consensus-facilitating middle ground. The world that today's students are growing up in and that they will soon enter into as active and engaged citizens is deeply fragmented in just this way. Issues relating to terrorism, immigration, women's rights, minority rights, race relations, health care, taxation, wealth and poverty, the environment, policing, military intervention, the proper role of government—in some ways, perennial issues that are freshly and uniquely urgent and vital with each new generation—are currently roiling the world.

If we are to foster a knowledgeable, responsible, active, and engaged citizenry among today's youth, we must provide them with the intellectual, interpretive, and critical-thinking tools and experience necessary to make sense of the world around them and of the all-important debates and arguments that inform it. After all, the outcome of these debates will in large measure determine the future course, prospects, and outcomes of the world and its peoples, particularly its youth. If they are to become successful members of society and productive and informed citizens, students need to learn how to evaluate the strengths and weaknesses of someone else's arguments, how to sift fact from opinion and fallacy, and how to test the relative merits and validity of their own opinions against the known facts and the best possible available information. The landmark series Opposing Viewpoints has been providing students with just such critical-thinking skills and exposure to the debates surrounding society's most urgent contemporary issues for many years, and it continues to serve this essential role with undiminished commitment, care, and rigor.

The key to the series' success in achieving its goal of sharpening students' critical-thinking and analytic skills resides in its title—

Opposing Viewpoints. In every intriguing, compelling, and engaging volume of this series, readers are presented with the widest possible spectrum of distinct viewpoints, expert opinions, and informed argumentation and commentary, supplied by some of today's leading academics, thinkers, analysts, politicians, policy makers, economists, activists, change agents, and advocates. Every opinion and argument anthologized here is presented objectively and accorded respect. There is no editorializing in any introductory text or in the arrangement and order of the pieces. No piece is included as a "straw man," an easy ideological target for cheap point-scoring. As wide and inclusive a range of viewpoints as possible is offered, with no privileging of one particular political ideology or cultural perspective over another. It is left to each individual reader to evaluate the relative merits of each argument—as he or she sees it, and with the use of ever-growing critical-thinking skills—and grapple with his or her own assumptions, beliefs, and perspectives to determine how convincing or successful any given argument is and how the reader's own stance on the issue may be modified or altered in response to it.

This process is facilitated and supported by volume, chapter, and selection introductions that provide readers with the essential context they need to begin engaging with the spotlighted issues, with the debates surrounding them, and with their own perhaps shifting or nascent opinions on them. In addition, guided reading and discussion questions encourage readers to determine the authors' point of view and purpose, interrogate and analyze the various arguments and their rhetoric and structure, evaluate the arguments' strengths and weaknesses, test their claims against available facts and evidence, judge the validity of the reasoning, and bring into clearer, sharper focus the readers' own beliefs and conclusions and how they may differ from or align with those in the collection or those of their classmates.

Research has shown that reading comprehension skills improve dramatically when students are provided with compelling, intriguing, and relevant "discussable" texts. The subject matter of these collections could not be more compelling, intriguing, or urgently relevant to today's students and the world they are poised to inherit. The anthologized articles and the reading and discussion questions that are included with them also provide the basis for stimulating, lively, and passionate classroom debates. Students who are compelled to anticipate objections to their own argument and identify the flaws in those of an opponent read more carefully, think more critically, and steep themselves in relevant context, facts, and information more thoroughly. In short, using discussable text of the kind provided by every single volume in the Opposing Viewpoints series encourages close reading, facilitates reading comprehension, fosters research, strengthens critical thinking, and greatly enlivens and energizes classroom discussion and participation. The entire learning process is deepened, extended, and strengthened.

For all of these reasons, Opposing Viewpoints continues to be exactly the right resource at exactly the right time—when we most need to provide readers with the critical-thinking tools and skills that will not only serve them well in school but also in their careers and their daily lives as decision-making family members, community members, and citizens. This series encourages respectful engagement with and analysis of opposing viewpoints and fosters a resulting increase in the strength and rigor of one's own opinions and stances. As such, it helps make readers "future ready," and that readiness will pay rich dividends for the readers themselves, for the citizenry, for our society, and for the world at large.

Introduction

> *"Were it left to me to decide whether*
> *we should have a government*
> *without newspapers, or newspapers*
> *without a government, I should*
> *not hesitate a moment to prefer*
> *the latter."*
>
> *—Thomas Jefferson on the*
> *importance of journalism*
> *to the health of the nation*

In one episode of the ground-breaking 1970s newsroom sitcom *The Mary Tyler Moore Show*, the staff's news director Lou Grant is told he must liven up his show with bantering and fluff stories. It is then that Grant utters three simple words in battling back against the edict that reflect even more on modern times than it did in the early 1970s. "News is truth," he said.

The distinction today is not so much about disseminating the important issues in the United States. It is more a matter of distinguishing between truthful and slanted journalism. The explosion of news sources in the era of Internet, cable television and social media has provided opportunities for anyone and everyone, even in the world of news, to express their opinions rather than report the facts in an unbiased fashion. Even cable news network CNN, considered at one time a bastion of unbiased reporting, has been criticized by the right for leaping to the left in its political coverage, particularly regarding President Donald Trump.

Trump, of course, is among the most polarizing figures in US history. The debate rages over whether news outlets such as CNN and dozens of others are simply reporting the news as created by a president who lies as a matter of course or are indeed prejudiced in their coverage. Every major and even minor source has received far greater scrutiny than ever before. Which ones have an agenda? Regardless, all of them rely on ratings and clicks and ad sales. It is in their best interest to publish first and correct any errors later.

Meanwhile, politicians are doing what they've always done—playing up to the media to gain favor and positive reporting. They were forced to work hard to do so in the days when viewers could choose only from three television networks and a few hometown newspapers. Though there were exceptions, such as former vice-president Spiro Agnew claiming that the media was slanted, the general consensus was that the American media remained basically unbiased. Not anymore. It is understood that hundreds of outlets indeed boast an agenda, including major cable networks such Fox News on the right and MSNBC on the left. That makes it far easier for politicians to get their messages across. But is it healthy for America? Was Lou Grant naive when he stated plainly that "news is truth"? And is anything besides unvarnished truth not news at all?

However that is answered, the problem to many has become a weakening of American journalism. It does not take a media critic to understand that those with an agenda are not seeking the truth. They are not tied to the journalistic ethic of searching for the truth on which a free press is based. They are only interested in furthering a narrative that indeed fits the agenda. That allows politicians to benefit from such media outlets while remaining unworried about illegal activities or, at the very least, ties to special interests, especially in their relationships with new sources that agree with their points of view.

Such is not always the case. Though the old-school network news shows have also been charged with bias, they have certainly received far less criticism than the hundreds of cable, Internet and social media outlets that have placed themselves into the media mainstream. The networks have indeed generally sought to maintain an ethical and impartial approach to news-gathering and reporting. Yet this day and age of Trump, a president who cries

"Fake News!" at unflattering stories and who has been accused by even his supporters of uttering daily untruths, has resulted in what some perceive as negative reporting simply based on those lies. The boundary between truths and lies in American journalism has become more blurred with time, especially since the 2016 presidential campaign was launched. In short, Trump changed everything.

Many people believe that the media requires a long, hard look at itself in a figurative mirror. It must return to its roots and understand its overwhelming importance to society and the health of the nation, especially in its political reporting. Only then will politicians be held to higher standards while catering less to special interests and more to their constituencies.

Other moral issues facing the political world are less tied to journalistic ethics and more tethered to the system. The question of term limits has been raised for generations. On one hand is the argument that limiting terms for those in the Senate and House of Representatives will in turn limit the affect of special interests on their actions. Those that know they cannot be reelected have no reason to allow powerful special interest groups such as the National Rifle Association dictate their actions. On the other hand, why should honest, hard-working and effective leaders, as well as their supporters, be punished via term limits? Would it not water down the field? Why would prospective and promising politicians even pursue a career in the knowledge that it could not continue?

In some way, times ways have not changed. There are honest politicians and crooked ones. But the ability and willingness of all in the American media to faithfully, strongly and in an unbiased manner learn and reveal the truth about them has changed. This has altered the relationships between politics and journalism. In chapters titled "Is the Post-Truth World a Permanent Reality?" "How Secure Is the Politician-Media Marriage?" "Is There a Place for Morals in Politics Today?" and "Are Special Interests Corrupting

Politics?" the contributors in *Opposing Viewpoints: Politics and Journalism in a Post-Truth World* explore the many facets of this issue. An ongoing examination of those relationships is necessary for both the media and political world to regain a balance in which both are operating separately and honestly. Our nation's founders would not have wanted it any other way.

OPPOSING
VIEWPOINTS®
SERIES

CHAPTER 1

Is the Post-Truth World a Permanent Reality?

Chapter Preface

D ishonest politicians have been a world reality for centuries. Politicians seeking election or reelection often lie as a matter of course to sway voters. Such tactics have remained the fodder for discussion and humor in the United States since George Washington was president. The result is a game that has been played forever between politicians and the media, which had worked together greatly in concert to separate fact from fiction.

Times have undeniably changed. There is little doubt, especially among cable television, Internet and social media outlets, that many in the media embrace agendas that slant the news. That allows politicians to seek out those that will not only accept, but even give credence to, the lies they yearn for the public to believe.

The result is a widening divide among Americans. They watch or listen to whatever media outlet feeds into their personal opinions and ignore the rest. They believe whatever politicians spew narratives that fit their views and call those on the other side of the aisle liars. There is little middle ground anymore.

The question then becomes whether this is the new permanent reality. The days of limited media are certainly over. Gone is the era of three television networks, daily newspapers and a few news magazines as the only news competition. That competition was based on the search for truth. The public read and watched and listened based on the ability of those media outlets to disseminate and report the news most efficiently and effectively. The sheer number of news distributors in the modern era preclude any possibility that all of them will ever be unbiased. But can media watchdogs make the American public more aware of such dishonesty and lure them toward balanced reporting? Lower ratings among politically skewed outlets could certainly motivate positive change.

> *"Lying by political leaders is what we expect from totalitarians. Free societies require truth and honesty."*

Politicians Lie to Us Every Day

Allan H. Meltzer

The greater willingness of politicians to lie not only on the campaign trail, but once in office, is the focus of the following viewpoint, which was written by former economic historian and policy expert Allan H. Meltzer. Meltzer, who won a Truman Medal in 2011 for his work in economic policy, argues that much work must be done to bring a stronger sense of truth back to politics in a wide range of issues. He does not cite one party or the other in his criticism, but rather the mindset of American politicians in general.

As you read, consider the following questions:

1. Does the author make clear his contention that political lying has expanded beyond campaigning and into policy?
2. What solutions does Meltzer suggest in making positive changes?
3. What issues does the author cite in pointing out how politicians in recent years have lied about policy matters?

Most of us learn at some point that politicians tell lies. We expect them to stop once they hold office or to face the consequences. In the past, politicians that violated the public trust resigned, most notably President Richard Nixon. Other lesser officials have also been punished for abusing public trust. No longer. In campaigns, and in office, politicians and their aides or supporters deliberately lie about matters of importance.

Ben Rhodes, a National Security Adviser in the Obama administration, bragged recently about the lies officials told to support a major foreign policy decision—the nuclear agreement with Iran. That agreement permits Iran to possess nuclear weapons in about ten years. Rhodes publicly admitted that the Obama administration claimed that the new Iranian government was a moderating influence despite the fact that experts at the Central Intelligence Agency warned that the new government in Iran was not moderate. According to Rhodes, that false claim was critical for getting the deal approved by Congress. He and his colleagues suffered no consequence for having lied.

The Obama administration lied to change a major foreign policy issue. Other lies are about less important but not unimportant issues. The French economist Thomas Piketty claimed that capitalism squeezes the middle and lower classes to favor the rich. Piketty's book *Capital in the Twenty-First Century* and other studies that followed supported that argument by relying on deceptive data—specifically, income before taxes and transfers. Critics pointed out that the case is much weaker if income after taxes and transfers is used, as it should be. That's much closer to the receipts that people have. And the differences are large. Transfers that are not part of income before taxes amount to more than $1 billion annually. The top 20 percent of taxpayers paid 84 percent of all income taxes in recent years. And the derided top 1 percent paid 23.5 percent of the income tax.

The failure to use income after taxes and transfers cannot be accidental. It seems to be a deliberate attempt to mislead the public. And it is not the only misuse of data. Much of the recent large rise in the income received by the top 1 or 10 percent results from the Federal Reserve's policy of lowering interest rates and raising housing and stock prices. Higher stock prices increase the incomes of those who own shares. Middle-income earners do not have large stock or bond portfolios. Their shares are mainly part of corporate pension plans. The rise in stock prices benefits the middle class by increasing the support for their future pensions. But the gain is part of their wealth and not part of their current income. So the rise in stock prices widens the spread in the income distribution and contributes to the clamor. That's measurement with little or no substantive effect.

Further, everyone has heard for years that middle class incomes have stalled. Is it true? A recent study by economists at the San Francisco Federal Reserve Bank shows that changes in the median wage are pulled down by the retirement of older workers and their replacement by less experienced younger workers. That study removes much of the issue. Expect it to be ignored. The San Francisco Reserve Bank also found that 69 percent of households surveyed in 2015 said they were "living comfortably." That's an increase from the 62 percent found in 2013. That doesn't support the widespread claim of system failure. Expect that to be ignored also.

Misleading and incorrect conclusions about income distribution are used to support political demands for increased tax rates on high incomes to redistribute more to others. That's bad advice. The long history of US growth shows that the middle class gains when their productivity increases. And that depends on investment, so reduced tax rates enhance productivity growth by increasing investment. And higher taxes on the groups that save and invest lower investment and productivity.

To expose this lie, politicians can have their staff look at the many stagnant or failing countries—Greece, Argentina, Venezuela, France, and Italy—where anti-capitalist policies have been tried and failed. We should not want to join them.

Hillary Clinton proclaims almost daily that women receive only 78 percent of the income that men receive. Her message is so misleading as to be dishonest. The 78 percent number is the ratio of women's to men's median pay. It does not adjust for occupational and other differences in the work that men and women do. For example, skilled neurosurgeons and football, baseball, and basketball stars are men. Domestic workers and hospital cleaning crews are mainly women. A recent paper by Diana Furchtgott-Roth summarized studies at Cornell and other quality economic departments. When adjustment for occupational differences are considered, the ratio is 92 or 94 percent, not the advertised 78 percent. And the remaining difference may not be due to discrimination. Differences in time in the work force, hours worked, and other factors may play a role.

Two striking facts stand out. The first is that laws require equal pay for equal work. Clinton's claim that there is great discrimination means that many employers violate the law with impunity. That's very implausible. Even journalists should be able to understand that. Second, the difference between 78 percent and 92 percent is well known to labor economists and almost certainly to some economists on Clinton's staff. Do they not tell her? Or does she not want to correct this central message of her campaign?

Economic growth is a major issue in this presidential campaign. Research has done much to uncover the factors that contribute to growth. Secure property rights, rule of law, open markets, and limited trade restrictions all play important roles. But the Trump and Clinton campaign messages are all critical of freer trade. It is false—a lie—to claim that freer trade has hurt us as a nation, as my Hoover colleague David Henderson has pointed out.

It has always been true that some lose as a result of trade agreements. We gave up textile jobs to gain jobs elsewhere, in services for example. Trade agreements including NAFTA raised income in the aggregate and provided some of the funding for retraining displaced workers. Trump is wrong or badly advised to oppose trade agreements and Clinton was badly advised when she shifted her position on the Pacific trade agreement. Of course, the agreements are complicated, so it is always possible to claim that a better agreement for the United States is possible—but it's not accurate to claim that trade restrictions will benefit Americans.

These are just a few examples of lies and misleading statements that we encounter every day. Clinton lies frequently and Trump shouts a falsehood a day—and probably more—as a major part of his campaign. This is not what citizens of a free country should expect and demand. And these examples are part of a much larger set.

At one time, citizens could count on their officials and candidates to either tell the truth or say nothing. Not any more. Clinton has a long record of neglecting truth. Trump seems not to care about the veracity of his statements. And the media is so much on one side that it mainly looks at the Trump gaffes and does its best to ignore Clinton's. And most serious of all, it allows the Obama administration to tell the public lies like Americans can keep their health insurance or that global warming is a coming disaster.

No less serious is the failure of politicians to tell us the truth about the promises that they have made that cannot be honored. Careful studies put the cost of government promises for pensions and future healthcare benefits at more than $100 trillion. There is no way that anything close to that amount will be available.

An honest government and honest candidates would inform the public about these truths and lead open discussions of what might be done. The fact that no candidate mentions that governments have promised more healthcare and pension spending than we can pay for tells us a great deal about the state of truth in government and among the candidates for the presidency.

Lying by political leaders is what we expect from totalitarians. Free societies require truth and honesty.

> *"At these times, the least journalists can offer is honesty, transparency and openness—the bare minimum if we are to make sense of the world and build trust that will allow people to tell their stories."*

The 24-Hour News Cycle Can Be Detrimental

Iman Amrani

In the following viewpoint Iman Amrani uses her personal experiences to provide an idealistic viewpoint about the power and purpose of journalists around the world. Specializing on issues of identity, race, and politics, the author argues that the news media must begin living up to higher standards. She expresses her views through one journey over a news cycle in which various issues were raised. Iman Amrani is an award-winning video journalist producing material for the Guardian, *having also contributed to many other news outlets.*

"Reporting on 2017: 'The Editor Had Never Seen A News Cycle Like This,'" by Iman Amrani, Guardian News and Media Limited, December 16, 2017. Reprinted by permission.

As you read, consider the following questions:

1. How did the author use her personal experiences to make a point about the obligation of the media?
2. How can one compare the current state of international news reporting to American journalism based on the following viewpoint?
3. Did the personal views of Iman Amrani make her unreasonably biased in presenting her case?

Growing up, news headlines often seemed disconnected from my lived experience. Important voices were spoken over or edited out and the rise of social media left little room for reflection. I became a journalist out of curiosity, and a desire to shine a spotlight on dark places and amplify different voices.

Chance and good timing have allowed me to begin my career in that direction. Since graduating in 2014, I have reported on terrorist attacks across Europe and covered knife crime and immigration in the UK. Some questions have been answered but more often than not they have multiplied. This year, against the backdrop of news shaking the world daily, I have continued to ask myself how I can add something constructive to the coverage—and 2017 has been a huge learning curve.

The day after Donald Trump's inauguration as US president, I covered the Women's March on London with three female colleagues. Between 80,000 and 100,000 people took to the streets to support women's rights, as sister marches happened all over the world. We knew it was an important moment—the Facebook Live footage we streamed from the march was viewed more than a million times—but on a personal level it also felt important to be on the ground, present in that moment.

A week or so later, Trump's "Muslim ban" triggered further protests; I remember wondering whether the momentum could be maintained. The underlying issues behind these protests felt personal in this increasingly globalised world.

Trump's rise to power when read alongside the Brexit referendum result led pundits to consider whether the spring might bring a shock victory for Marine Le Pen. For a few weeks all eyes were on France, and I headed to Marseille to report on the fractures in French society. Following an intense election, I decided to keep my head down over the summer, establish a quieter routine over the period of Ramadan and take time to develop some new stories.

A week before Ramadan, the Manchester Arena was attacked. Young girls attending a concert by Ariana Grande were targeted and killed by a young British Libyan suicide bomber. I had reported from Paris and Brussels after other terrorist attacks, so I set off for Manchester.

There, the media circus seemed inescapable. But press conferences and camera scrums aren't the places where the most important stories are happening, and I wanted to try to understand what the attack meant to people. My mum phoned to ask how things were going. She grew up in Manchester, met my father at the university and got married at Didsbury mosque, the focus of the news that week.

I asked my editor for time to cover the story sensitively. I heard whispers from people in the Libyan community, but immediately after the attack, many were not yet ready to speak. We decided I would go back to Manchester when the circus had died down to deal with some of the questions still unanswered.

The following Saturday, I was shooting a piece about youth engagement in politics at a Grime4Corbyn event. I had interviewed Jeremy Corbyn when he was running for Labour leader and genuinely thought that the buzz around him would translate to some votes even though older, more established journalists didn't believe it.

I was backstage with Alex, a friend and journalist for a leading international news agency, when he got a phonecall. "Suspected terrorist attack, London Bridge," he said, swiftly packing his camera kit into his rucksack. "I have to go, I'm on call and there's no one else in London tonight."

There was no way he could carry his gear by himself, and he needed an assistant producer. "I'm coming with you," I said, heaving the bags into the boot of his car.

We drove towards London Bridge, then from Liverpool Street we had to make our way towards Borough Market on foot, through crowds of panicked people. At one point we were caught inside a cordon, with dozens of armed police in combat helmets marching at the end of the deserted street. Alex warned me not to run; from a distance the tripod and rucksack might look suspicious to the armed police.

I'd be lying if I said I wasn't scared. But we had a job to do and not a lot of time. At about 5am, after Alex shot footage that would be used by TV channels across the world, I left to go home to bed.

Later, when I woke, the horror of it all grew. Details and numbers of casualties mounted. Messages came through from friends around the world, checking I was safe.

The UK general election happened just a few days later. And yes, young people did make their voices heard in polling stations and, as a result, newsrooms. Friends expressed triumphant feelings about what had happened on the political scene.

Those feelings were quickly forgotten days later when the country woke to the news that a tower block in West London was on fire. An unknown number of people and their families had died.

That morning I went down to Grenfell to cover events. As in Manchester, I felt acutely aware this was a community where people were in shock. I drew back from mourning relatives, trying to respect their privacy. But I also wanted to find a way to use my role as a journalist to support those affected.

By the weekend the anger was visible. It appeared that no authority was taking responsibility. Information was slow to be released. Theresa May's fleeting visit left a bitter taste.

I went to an open meeting at the mosque set up for victims of the fire. The room was full of people who had lost everything and couldn't even hold funerals.

I stood in that mosque in the middle of Ramadan, feeling utterly helpless. I couldn't pretend this wasn't happening in our city. I just needed time to find a way to tell some truth about these events while respecting people who were sick of predatory journalists trying to capture suffering on camera.

My colleagues and I were exhausted. The *Guardian* doesn't have a huge team of video producers, like some of the broadcasters, but everyone was doing their best. Sunday was Father's Day, and one colleague left his son at home to come and work. He had previously covered conflict zones in the Middle East. I took him to where the cameras were lined up filming the ruins of Grenfell. We were next to the church and flowers were still being laid. The sound of the congregation singing hymns came through the open windows. I turned and saw he was crying.

Later that day I interviewed a local artist, AJ Tracey, and his brother Mickey, two young men who were part of the community, but had enough distance to be able to express some of the emotions that were bubbling in the area. If I did nothing else, I knew amplifying these voices was the best thing I could do for now.

Completely drained, I was sent home in a taxi by my editor late that night. Twenty minutes later I heard helicopters overhead. Reports were coming in that a car had driven into a crowd leaving a mosque in Finsbury Park. That's close to my sister's house, just down the road from me. She wasn't answering her phone. I asked the driver to take me as close as he could.

I saw armed police. It felt like deja vu—the same uniforms and helmets I'd seen a few weeks earlier at London Bridge. My only concern was for my sister: I pushed past the police cordon, rushed to her house, and hammered on the front door. She finally opened it, rubbing her eyes; she had been sleeping, unaware of events down the road. Relief swept over me. I hugged her, sent a quick video of the scene to the office, and went home to bed.

The following day, in the office, the *Guardian*'s deputy editor said that throughout his whole career he had never seen a news cycle like this. That felt reassuring in a way. There's a bit of a taboo around talking about stress in journalism—you don't want to be seen as too sensitive for the job—so his recognition that these were exceptional circumstances felt important.

My editor insisted I didn't change my imminent plans to spend Eid with my family in Algeria, so I went to Oran, my father's home city, for two weeks. It was only when I got there that I realised how stressful things had been over the last months. Priorities were put into perspective. I felt lucky to be able to watch my grandmother make cous cous; I appreciated sitting in my uncle's car by the sea listening to music on the radio; I enjoyed staying up late laughing with my cousins.

I thought about all the families back in the UK, affected by the events that had rocked the country over the summer. The nurses, doctors, firefighters, police, volunteers and members of the public who were on the frontline. The people who stepped up and stepped in and barely had the time to process one thing before another happened.

At these times, the least journalists can offer is honesty, transparency and openness—the bare minimum if we are to make sense of the world and build trust that will allow people to tell their stories.

I hope that I'll be able to continue striving for that in 2018, whatever it brings.

"The problem is not presidential
re-election. The problem
is presidentialism."

Presidents Have Too Much Power

Patricio Navia

In the following viewpoint Patricio Navia argues against term limits.
The author makes his case with examples taken from his experiences
in Latin America, but his views can give Americans food for thought.
It is the author's view that lessening the power of the presidency
while allowing those in office to remain there as long as they win
elections creates the healthiest political process. Patricio Navia serves
as a contributing columnist for Americas Quarterly *and is professor*
of liberal studies at New York University and of political science at
Diego Portales University of Chile.

As you read, consider the following questions:

1. Can one legitimately compare the viability of term limits
   in Latin America and the United States?
2. Did the author make his arguments against term limits
   clear and concise?
3. Why does the author believe democracy is being
   compromised in Latin America?

"Limit the Power of Presidents, Not Their Term in Office," by Patricio Navia, Americas Quarterly, March-June 2009. Reprinted by permission.

L et them run. The problem is not presidential re-election. The problem is presidentialism.

As long as Latin American democracies continue to be based on institutional arrangements—both formal and informal—that concentrate power in the executive, democratic development will be undermined. This concentration of power carries the seeds of instability that will hinder, if not reverse, democratic consolidation, regardless of whether presidential term limits are imposed. It underlines both the perils of authoritarianism and the lack of accountability that accompany governance in the region.

In recent months, the debate over presidential re-election has been fueled by the open effort to eliminate term limits championed by Venezuelan President Hugo Chávez and the more concealed campaign by Colombian President Álvaro Uribe to do the same. Recent constitutional assemblies in Ecuador and Bolivia have set presidential re-election limits at two terms, following a trend that began with then-President Alberto Fujimori's interpretation of the 1993 Peruvian constitution. Subsequent reforms in Argentina in 1994 and in Brazil, under the first Fernando Henrique Cardoso administration (1994–98), consolidated the trend. Today, the practice of limiting leaders to two consecutive terms has extended to all major countries in the region, with the notable exceptions of Mexico and Chile. In most countries—except for Mexico and Costa Rica—term limits do not generally apply to legislators or to local and provincial officeholders. (Venezuela eliminated them with its recent referendum.)

To be sure, allowing officeholders other than the executive to seek re-election is generally seen as a good and convenient feature in well-functioning democracies. It increases responsiveness and places the correct incentives on officeholders to be accountable to their constituents. Without the possibility of re-election, representatives lack the incentive to serve those who voted them in. The prospect of re-election implies that representatives can be "fired" by constituents who feel they have not been served well. Efforts to introduce term limits were initially framed as promoting responsiveness. But it turns out that they do not have a significant effect in limiting political careers: officeholders who are term-limited simply switch to other elected positions to continue their careers. Nor do they bring about a renewal of the political elite, since many local political bosses turn to their relatives to fill their places or have stand-ins elected to occupy their seats until they are allowed to run again.

There are better mechanisms to promote accountability and responsiveness. Rather than preventing people from running, reformers should promote institutional changes that foster competition, lower entry thresholds for new challengers and level the playing field in campaign spending. In short, rather than prohibiting a television series, regardless of its popularity, from going into a new season, the best way to promote better television is by facilitating competition among different networks. Television series will survive if they can withstand competition from new challengers. By forcing a television series off the air because it has been on the air too long, we will not automatically produce better-quality television. The same applies to politics.

True, individual politicians are not the only actors interested in serving constituents well. Political parties also have those incentives. In a healthy democracy with strong and accountable parties, if individual officeholders are not allowed to run for re-election, the political parties they represent have every incentive to make sure their representatives do a good job. Otherwise, the parties will be punished when voters go to the polls.

Unfortunately, Latin American countries have notoriously weak party systems. Thus, voters often have few tools at their disposal to punish and reward incumbents other than the threat or benefit of re-election. This is particularly true for presidents who run as independents. If re-election is impossible, independent presidents have no incentive to fulfill their campaign promises. Even worse, voters have no way to punish independent presidents who are banned from seeking re-election.

The debate about presidential term limits in Latin America is a remake of the debate over presidentialism and parliamentarism. Advocates of the parliamentary system argued 20 years ago that

ARE TERM LIMITS A VIABLE ANSWER?

In an American society increasingly polarized over politics, one uniting belief is that there is something very wrong with our government. While this is true, there is an unfortunate tendency on both sides—to try to identify simple, easy to recite reforms to fix our woes.

On the left, for example, the cries are usually for "getting money out of politics," with various organizations pushing to "repeal" the Citizens United ruling. On the right, it is common to see calls for a Federal balanced-budget amendment and term limits. While there's certainly no harm in preventing the Federal government from running up deficits—though the issue is more complicated than many realize the call for term limits is every bit as misguided as the left's call for restricting campaign funds. It misidentifies the underlying issue and would actually manage to make the Federal government even more immune from voter accountability.

One point in term limits' favor is that they are popular. Polling in recent years indicates that term limits are supported by up to 75% of the country, which explains why they were included in the platforms of various presidential candidates. The popularity can probably be chalked up both to its simplicity, and to the fact that few groups are hated quite as much as the US Congress has been in recent history.

There is certainly something said for "throwing the bums out," but failing to address the more fundamental problems with the Federal government would likely find voters similarly dissatisfied in short order. This is the main fallacy of term limits: it presumes the problem is the people in government, and not the government itself.

After all, America was given a taste of what a "fresh" Congress would look like following the Tea Party wave of 2010. The 112th Congress had more new members than any class in over 60 years, with almost a full quarter of the body made up of freshmen. Six years later, Congress functions much as it did prior to the influx of new legislators—with even the trademark issue of runaway government spending fading into a political afterthought.

Why is this? The simple truth is that most people overestimate the power of individual elected officials and underestimate the influence of the professional political class.

"Are Term Limits A Solution?" by Tho Bishop, Mises Institute, October 5, 2016.

Latin American democracies organized on a presidential basis are inherently unstable, since they concentrate too much power in one person. If that argument is accepted, allowing presidents to seek additional terms would clearly worsen the situation.

Yet when you get lemons, you might as well try to make lemonade. The drive in favor of allowing unlimited re-election for presidents in Latin America should be used to curtail the powers and attributions of presidents. When leaders such as Hugo Chávez press for unlimited re-election, citing the examples of France, the United Kingdom or Germany, pro-democracy advocates should respond by calling for constitutional reforms that, while letting presidents run for re-election indefinitely, also introduce better checks and balances that actually undermine the strength of the president, such as removing their control over the legislative agenda and by limiting government by decree and discretionary power over spending. Thus, Chávez will have the same ability as a German chancellor to run for office as many times as he likes, but his executive powers will be limited just as they are in Germany.

Latin American democracies suffer from lack of competition. Individuals or political parties tend to promote monopolies and oligopolies that undermine it. Political parties favor high entry barriers to prevent new parties from challenging their oligopoly control. Individual politicians in congress make it difficult for newcomers to challenge them by enacting complex and opaque campaign finance rules—which in many cases directly favor incumbents.

The push to eliminate presidential term limits should be seen as a symptom of an ill-functioning democracy, rather than its cause. It would be wiser, therefore, to fight the disease itself, not the symptoms. Term-limited presidents already exercise too much power. Rather than replacing one overly powerful president with another equally powerful one, it would make more sense to reduce the powers and attributions of the presidency regardless of who occupies the office. Let them run as often as they wish, but make races more competitive, level the playing field and reduce the powers and attributions of the president.

> " *The majority of politicians, on the evidence available to us, are interested not in truth but in power and in the maintenance of that power. To maintain that power it is essential that people ... live in ignorance of the truth, even the truth of their own lives.*"

The Search for the Truth Can Never Stop

Harold Pinter

In the following viewpoint, an excerpted transcript of a Nobel Lecture, Harold Pinter delves into the political arena by comparing the world in which he worked well over a half-century ago to the political oratory on the current American stage. The author argues that lies spewed forth by current politicians are far too accepted by the public and that such mistruths keep people in the dark, which is where the powers-that-be prefer wants them. Pinter is particularly critical of the penchant of politicians to lie about foreign affairs that maintain their power and the military and economic power of the country. Harold Pinter was a Nobel Prize-winning British playwright.

"Harold Pinter—Nobel Lecture," by Harold Pinter, ©The Nobel Foundation, 2005. Reprinted by permission.

As you read, consider the following questions:

1. What foreign entanglements does the author cite in calling out American politicians for their lies?
2. How does the author analogize his thoughts about his work as a playwright to the words and actions of politicians?
3. Does the author consider some American politicians to be criminals?

I n 1958 I wrote the following:

> There are no hard distinctions between what is real and what is unreal, nor between what is true and what is false. A thing is not necessarily either true or false; it can be both true and false.

I believe that these assertions still make sense and do still apply to the exploration of reality through art. So as a writer I stand by them but as a citizen I cannot. As a citizen I must ask: What is true? What is false?

Truth in drama is forever elusive. You never quite find it but the search for it is compulsive. The search is clearly what drives the endeavour. The search is your task. More often than not you stumble upon the truth in the dark, colliding with it or just glimpsing an image or a shape which seems to correspond to the truth, often without realising that you have done so. But the real truth is that there never is any such thing as one truth to be found in dramatic art. There are many. These truths challenge each other, recoil from each other, reflect each other, ignore each other, tease each other, are blind to each other. Sometimes you feel you have the truth of a moment in your hand, then it slips through your fingers and is lost.

I have often been asked how my plays come about. I cannot say. Nor can I ever sum up my plays, except to say that this is what happened. That is what they said. That is what they did.

Most of the plays are engendered by a line, a word or an image. The given word is often shortly followed by the image. I shall give two examples of two lines which came right out of the blue into my head, followed by an image, followed by me.

The plays are *The Homecoming* and *Old Times*. The first line of *The Homecoming* is "What have you done with the scissors?" The first line of *Old Times* is "Dark."

In each case I had no further information.

In the first case someone was obviously looking for a pair of scissors and was demanding their whereabouts of someone else he suspected had probably stolen them. But I somehow knew that the person addressed didn't give a damn about the scissors or about the questioner either, for that matter.

"Dark" I took to be a description of someone's hair, the hair of a woman, and was the answer to a question. In each case I found myself compelled to pursue the matter. This happened visually, a very slow fade, through shadow into light.

I always start a play by calling the characters A, B and C.

In the play that became *The Homecoming* I saw a man enter a stark room and ask his question of a younger man sitting on an ugly sofa reading a racing paper. I somehow suspected that A was a father and that B was his son, but I had no proof. This was however confirmed a short time later when B (later to become Lenny) says to A (later to become Max), "Dad, do you mind if I change the subject? I want to ask you something. The dinner we had before, what was the name of it? What do you call it? Why don't you buy a dog? You're a dog cook. Honest. You think you're cooking for a lot of dogs." So since B calls A "Dad" it seemed to me reasonable to assume that they were father and son. A was also clearly the cook and his cooking did not seem to be held in high regard. Did this mean that there was no mother? I didn't know. But, as I told myself at the time, our beginnings never know our ends.

"Dark." A large window. Evening sky. A man, A (later to become Deeley), and a woman, B (later to become Kate), sitting with drinks. "Fat or thin?" the man asks. Who are they talking about? But I then see, standing at the window, a woman, C (later to become Anna), in another condition of light, her back to them, her hair dark.

It's a strange moment, the moment of creating characters who up to that moment have had no existence. What follows is fitful, uncertain, even hallucinatory, although sometimes it can be an unstoppable avalanche. The author's position is an odd one. In a sense he is not welcomed by the characters. The characters resist him, they are not easy to live with, they are impossible to define. You certainly can't dictate to them. To a certain extent you play a never-ending game with them, cat and mouse, blind man's buff, hide and seek. But finally you find that you have people of flesh and blood on your hands, people with will and an individual sensibility of their own, made out of component parts you are unable to change, manipulate or distort.

So language in art remains a highly ambiguous transaction, a quicksand, a trampoline, a frozen pool which might give way under you, the author, at any time.

But as I have said, the search for the truth can never stop. It cannot be adjourned, it cannot be postponed. It has to be faced, right there, on the spot.

Political theatre presents an entirely different set of problems. Sermonising has to be avoided at all cost. Objectivity is essential. The characters must be allowed to breathe their own air. The author cannot confine and constrict them to satisfy his own taste or disposition or prejudice. He must be prepared to approach them from a variety of angles, from a full and uninhibited range of perspectives, take them by surprise, perhaps, occasionally, but nevertheless give them the freedom to go which way they will. This does not always work. And political satire, of course, adheres to none of these precepts, in fact does precisely the opposite, which is its proper function.

In my play *The Birthday Party* I think I allow a whole range of options to operate in a dense forest of possibility before finally focussing on an act of subjugation.

Mountain Language pretends to no such range of operation. It remains brutal, short and ugly. But the soldiers in the play do get some fun out of it. One sometimes forgets that torturers become easily bored. They need a bit of a laugh to keep their spirits up. This has been confirmed of course by the events at Abu Ghraib in Baghdad. *Mountain Language* lasts only 20 minutes, but it could go on for hour after hour, on and on and on, the same pattern repeated over and over again, on and on, hour after hour.

Ashes to Ashes, on the other hand, seems to me to be taking place under water. A drowning woman, her hand reaching up through the waves, dropping down out of sight, reaching for others, but finding nobody there, either above or under the water, finding only shadows, reflections, floating; the woman a lost figure in a drowning landscape, a woman unable to escape the doom that seemed to belong only to others.

But as they died, she must die too.

Political language, as used by politicians, does not venture into any of this territory since the majority of politicians, on the evidence available to us, are interested not in truth but in power and in the maintenance of that power. To maintain that power it is essential that people remain in ignorance, that they live in ignorance of the truth, even the truth of their own lives. What surrounds us therefore is a vast tapestry of lies, upon which we feed.

As every single person here knows, the justification for the invasion of Iraq was that Saddam Hussein possessed a highly dangerous body of weapons of mass destruction, some of which could be fired in 45 minutes, bringing about appalling devastation. We were assured that was true. It was not true. We were told that Iraq had a relationship with Al Quaeda and shared responsibility for the atrocity in New York of September 11th 2001. We were assured that this was true. It was not true. We were told that Iraq threatened the security of the world. We were assured it was true. It was not true.

The truth is something entirely different. The truth is to do with how the United States understands its role in the world and how it chooses to embody it.

But before I come back to the present I would like to look at the recent past, by which I mean United States foreign policy since the end of the Second World War. I believe it is obligatory upon us to subject this period to at least some kind of even limited scrutiny, which is all that time will allow here.

Everyone knows what happened in the Soviet Union and throughout Eastern Europe during the post-war period: the systematic brutality, the widespread atrocities, the ruthless suppression of independent thought. All this has been fully documented and verified.

But my contention here is that the US crimes in the same period have only been superficially recorded, let alone documented, let alone acknowledged, let alone recognised as crimes at all. I believe this must be addressed and that the truth has considerable bearing on where the world stands now. Although constrained, to a certain extent, by the existence of the Soviet Union, the United States' actions throughout the world made it clear that it had concluded it had carte blanche to do what it liked.

Direct invasion of a sovereign state has never in fact been America's favoured method. In the main, it has preferred what it has described as "low intensity conflict." Low intensity conflict means that thousands of people die but slower than if you dropped a bomb on them in one fell swoop. It means that you infect the heart of the country, that you establish a malignant growth and watch the gangrene bloom. When the populace has been subdued— or beaten to death—the same thing—and your own friends, the military and the great corporations, sit comfortably in power, you go before the camera and say that democracy has prevailed. This was a commonplace in US foreign policy in the years to which I refer.

The tragedy of Nicaragua was a highly significant case. I choose to offer it here as a potent example of America's view of its role in the world, both then and now.

I was present at a meeting at the US embassy in London in the late 1980s.

The United States Congress was about to decide whether to give more money to the Contras in their campaign against the state of

Nicaragua. I was a member of a delegation speaking on behalf of Nicaragua but the most important member of this delegation was a Father John Metcalf. The leader of the US body was Raymond Seitz (then number two to the ambassador, later ambassador himself). Father Metcalf said: "Sir, I am in charge of a parish in the north of Nicaragua. My parishioners built a school, a health centre, a cultural centre. We have lived in peace. A few months ago a Contra force attacked the parish. They destroyed everything: the school, the health centre, the cultural centre. They raped nurses and teachers, slaughtered doctors, in the most brutal manner. They behaved like savages. Please demand that the US government withdraw its support from this shocking terrorist activity."

Raymond Seitz had a very good reputation as a rational, responsible and highly sophisticated man. He was greatly respected in diplomatic circles. He listened, paused and then spoke with some gravity. "Father," he said, "let me tell you something. In war, innocent people always suffer." There was a frozen silence. We stared at him. He did not flinch.

Innocent people, indeed, always suffer.

Finally somebody said: "But in this case 'innocent people' were the victims of a gruesome atrocity subsidised by your government, one among many. If Congress allows the Contras more money further atrocities of this kind will take place. Is this not the case? Is your government not therefore guilty of supporting acts of murder and destruction upon the citizens of a sovereign state?"

Seitz was imperturbable. "I don't agree that the facts as presented support your assertions," he said.

As we were leaving the Embassy a US aide told me that he enjoyed my plays. I did not reply.

I should remind you that at the time President Reagan made the following statement: "The Contras are the moral equivalent of our Founding Fathers."

The United States supported the brutal Somoza dictatorship in Nicaragua for over 40 years. The Nicaraguan people, led by the Sandinistas, overthrew this regime in 1979, a breathtaking popular revolution.

The Sandinistas weren't perfect. They possessed their fair share of arrogance and their political philosophy contained a number of contradictory elements. But they were intelligent, rational and civilised. They set out to establish a stable, decent, pluralistic society. The death penalty was abolished. Hundreds of thousands of poverty-stricken peasants were brought back from the dead. Over 100,000 families were given title to land. Two thousand schools were built. A quite remarkable literacy campaign reduced illiteracy in the country to less than one seventh. Free education was established and a free health service. Infant mortality was reduced by a third. Polio was eradicated.

The United States denounced these achievements as Marxist/Leninist subversion. In the view of the US government, a dangerous example was being set. If Nicaragua was allowed to establish basic norms of social and economic justice, if it was allowed to raise the standards of health care and education and achieve social unity and national self respect, neighbouring countries would ask the same questions and do the same things. There was of course at the time fierce resistance to the status quo in El Salvador.

I spoke earlier about "a tapestry of lies" which surrounds us. President Reagan commonly described Nicaragua as a "totalitarian dungeon." This was taken generally by the media, and certainly by the British government, as accurate and fair comment. But there was in fact no record of death squads under the Sandinista government. There was no record of torture. There was no record of systematic or official military brutality. No priests were ever murdered in Nicaragua. There were in fact three priests in the government, two Jesuits and a Maryknoll missionary. The totalitarian dungeons were actually next door, in El Salvador and Guatemala. The United States had brought down the democratically elected government of Guatemala in 1954 and it is estimated that over 200,000 people had been victims of successive military dictatorships.

Six of the most distinguished Jesuits in the world were viciously murdered at the Central American University in San Salvador in 1989 by a battalion of the Alcatl regiment trained at Fort Benning, Georgia, USA. That extremely brave man Archbishop Romero was assassinated while saying mass. It is estimated that 75,000 people died. Why were they killed? They were killed because they believed a better life was possible and should be achieved. That belief immediately qualified them as communists. They died because they dared to question the status quo, the endless plateau of poverty, disease, degradation and oppression, which had been their birthright.

The United States finally brought down the Sandinista government. It took some years and considerable resistance but relentless economic persecution and 30,000 dead finally undermined the spirit of the Nicaraguan people. They were exhausted and poverty stricken once again. The casinos moved back into the country. Free health and free education were over. Big business returned with a vengeance. "Democracy" had prevailed.

But this "policy" was by no means restricted to Central America. It was conducted throughout the world. It was never-ending. And it is as if it never happened.

The United States supported and in many cases engendered every right wing military dictatorship in the world after the end of the Second World War. I refer to Indonesia, Greece, Uruguay, Brazil, Paraguay, Haiti, Turkey, the Philippines, Guatemala, El Salvador, and, of course, Chile. The horror the United States inflicted upon Chile in 1973 can never be purged and can never be forgiven.

Hundreds of thousands of deaths took place throughout these countries. Did they take place? And are they in all cases attributable to US foreign policy? The answer is yes they did take place and they are attributable to American foreign policy. But you wouldn't know it.

It never happened. Nothing ever happened. Even while it was happening it wasn't happening. It didn't matter. It was of no interest.

The crimes of the United States have been systematic, constant, vicious, remorseless, but very few people have actually talked about them. You have to hand it to America. It has exercised a quite clinical manipulation of power worldwide while masquerading as a force for universal good. It's a brilliant, even witty, highly successful act of hypnosis.

I put to you that the United States is without doubt the greatest show on the road. Brutal, indifferent, scornful and ruthless it may be but it is also very clever. As a salesman it is out on its own and its most saleable commodity is self love. It's a winner. Listen to all American presidents on television say the words, "the American people," as in the sentence, "I say to the American people it is time to pray and to defend the rights of the American people and I ask the American people to trust their president in the action he is about to take on behalf of the American people."

It's a scintillating stratagem. Language is actually employed to keep thought at bay. The words "the American people" provide a truly voluptuous cushion of reassurance. You don't need to think. Just lie back on the cushion. The cushion may be suffocating your intelligence and your critical faculties but it's very comfortable. This does not apply of course to the 40 million people living below the poverty line and the 2 million men and women imprisoned in the vast gulag of prisons, which extends across the US.

The United States no longer bothers about low intensity conflict. It no longer sees any point in being reticent or even devious. It puts its cards on the table without fear or favour. It quite simply doesn't give a damn about the United Nations, international law or critical dissent, which it regards as impotent and irrelevant. It also has its own bleating little lamb tagging behind it on a lead, the pathetic and supine Great Britain.

What has happened to our moral sensibility? Did we ever have any? What do these words mean? Do they refer to a term very rarely employed these days—conscience? A conscience to do not only with our own acts but to do with our shared responsibility in the acts of others? Is all this dead? Look at Guantanamo Bay. Hundreds of people detained without charge for over three years, with no legal representation or due process, technically detained forever. This totally illegitimate structure is maintained in defiance of the Geneva Convention. It is not only tolerated but hardly thought about by what's called the "international community." This criminal outrage is being committed by a country, which declares itself to be "the leader of the free world." Do we think about the inhabitants of Guantanamo Bay? What does the media say about them? They pop up occasionally—a small item on page six. They have been consigned to a no man's land from which indeed they may never return. At present many are on hunger strike, being force-fed, including British residents. No niceties in these force-feeding procedures. No sedative or anaesthetic. Just a tube stuck up your nose and into your throat. You vomit blood. This is torture. What has the British Foreign Secretary said about this? Nothing. What has the British Prime Minister said about this? Nothing. Why not? Because the United States has said: to criticise our conduct in Guantanamo Bay constitutes an unfriendly act. You're either with us or against us. So Blair shuts up.

The invasion of Iraq was a bandit act, an act of blatant state terrorism, demonstrating absolute contempt for the concept of international law. The invasion was an arbitrary military action inspired by a series of lies upon lies and gross manipulation of the media and therefore of the public; an act intended to consolidate American military and economic control of the Middle East masquerading—as a last resort—all other justifications having failed to justify themselves—as liberation. A formidable assertion of military force responsible for the death and mutilation of thousands and thousands of innocent people.

We have brought torture, cluster bombs, depleted uranium, innumerable acts of random murder, misery, degradation and death to the Iraqi people and call it "bringing freedom and democracy to the Middle East."

How many people do you have to kill before you qualify to be described as a mass murderer and a war criminal? One hundred thousand? More than enough, I would have thought. Therefore it is just that Bush and Blair be arraigned before the International Criminal Court of Justice. But Bush has been clever. He has not ratified the International Criminal Court of Justice. Therefore if any American soldier or for that matter politician finds himself in the dock Bush has warned that he will send in the marines. But Tony Blair has ratified the Court and is therefore available for prosecution. We can let the Court have his address if they're interested. It is Number 10, Downing Street, London.

Death in this context is irrelevant. Both Bush and Blair place death well away on the back burner. At least 100,000 Iraqis were killed by American bombs and missiles before the Iraq insurgency began. These people are of no moment. Their deaths don't exist. They are blank. They are not even recorded as being dead. "We don't do body counts," said the American general Tommy Franks.

Early in the invasion there was a photograph published on the front page of British newspapers of Tony Blair kissing the cheek of a little Iraqi boy. "A grateful child," said the caption. A few days later there was a story and photograph, on an inside page, of another four-year-old boy with no arms. His family had been blown up by a missile. He was the only survivor. "When do I get my arms back?" he asked. The story was dropped. Well, Tony Blair wasn't holding him in his arms, nor the body of any other mutilated child, nor the body of any bloody corpse. Blood is dirty. It dirties your shirt and tie when you're making a sincere speech on television.

The 2,000 American dead are an embarrassment. They are transported to their graves in the dark. Funerals are unobtrusive, out of harm's way. The mutilated rot in their beds, some for the rest of their lives. So the dead and the mutilated both rot, in different kinds of graves.

[…]

I have said earlier that the United States is now totally frank about putting its cards on the table. That is the case. Its official declared policy is now defined as "full spectrum dominance." That is not my term, it is theirs. "Full spectrum dominance" means control of land, sea, air and space and all attendant resources.

The United States now occupies 702 military installations throughout the world in 132 countries, with the honourable exception of Sweden, of course. We don't quite know how they got there but they are there all right.

The United States possesses 8,000 active and operational nuclear warheads. Two thousand are on hair trigger alert, ready to be launched with 15 minutes warning. It is developing new systems of nuclear force, known as bunker busters. The British, ever cooperative, are intending to replace their own nuclear missile, Trident. Who, I wonder, are they aiming at? Osama bin Laden? You? Me? Joe Dokes? China? Paris? Who knows? What we do know is that this infantile insanity—the possession and threatened use of nuclear weapons—is at the heart of present American political philosophy. We must remind ourselves that the United States is on a permanent military footing and shows no sign of relaxing it.

Many thousands, if not millions, of people in the United States itself are demonstrably sickened, shamed and angered by their government's actions, but as things stand they are not a coherent political force—yet. But the anxiety, uncertainty and fear which we can see growing daily in the United States is unlikely to diminish.

I know that President Bush has many extremely competent speech writers but I would like to volunteer for the job myself. I propose the following short address which he can make on television to the nation. I see him grave, hair carefully combed, serious, winning, sincere, often beguiling, sometimes employing a wry smile, curiously attractive, a man's man.

"God is good. God is great. God is good. My God is good. Bin Laden's God is bad. His is a bad God. Saddam's God was bad, except he didn't have one. He was a barbarian. We are not barbarians. We don't chop people's heads off. We believe in freedom. So does God. I am not a barbarian. I am the democratically elected leader of a freedom-loving democracy. We are a compassionate society.

We give compassionate electrocution and compassionate lethal injection. We are a great nation. I am not a dictator. He is. I am not a barbarian. He is. And he is. They all are. I possess moral authority. You see this fist? This is my moral authority. And don't you forget it."

A writer's life is a highly vulnerable, almost naked activity. We don't have to weep about that. The writer makes his choice and is stuck with it. But it is true to say that you are open to all the winds, some of them icy indeed. You are out on your own, out on a limb. You find no shelter, no protection—unless you lie—in which case of course you have constructed your own protection and, it could be argued, become a politician.

I have referred to death quite a few times this evening. I shall now quote a poem of my own called "Death."

> Where was the dead body found?
> Who found the dead body?
> Was the dead body dead when found?
> How was the dead body found?
> Who was the dead body?
> Who was the father or daughter or brother
> Or uncle or sister or mother or son
> Of the dead and abandoned body?
> Was the body dead when abandoned?
> Was the body abandoned?
> By whom had it been abandoned?
> Was the dead body naked or dressed for a journey?
> What made you declare the dead body dead?
> Did you declare the dead body dead?
> How well did you know the dead body?
> How did you know the dead body was dead?
> Did you wash the dead body
> Did you close both its eyes
> Did you bury the body
> Did you leave it abandoned
> Did you kiss the dead body

When we look into a mirror we think the image that confronts us is accurate. But move a millimetre and the image changes. We are actually looking at a never-ending range of reflections. But sometimes a writer has to smash the mirror—for it is on the other side of that mirror that the truth stares at us.

I believe that despite the enormous odds which exist, unflinching, unswerving, fierce intellectual determination, as citizens, to define the real truth of our lives and our societies is a crucial obligation which devolves upon us all. It is in fact mandatory.

If such a determination is not embodied in our political vision we have no hope of restoring what is so nearly lost to us—the dignity of man.

> " 'Mainstream media' has changed
> from a general description into a
> term of abuse."

People No Longer Trust the Media

Andrew Harrison

In the following viewpoint Andrew Harrison argues that mistrust of the media is certainly not strictly an American issue. The author believes that mistrust is not based on a perception of "fake news," but rather a political slant. He expresses his view that a higher percentage of strong, knowledgeable, and unbiased journalists are needed in his country to counter the widespread feeling that the media is not doing its job. Harrison feels that British journalists simply must prove themselves to foster changes in perception. Andrew Harrison is a journalist whose work has appeared in the Guardian, *the* Observer, *and* New Statesman, *among many others.*

As you read, consider the following questions:

1. How does the author compare the "fake news" claims of US politicians to complaints in the UK?
2. Can you detect the author's feelings about how the British media has covered Brexit?
3. Does the relationship between UK politicians and the media appear different than in the US?

"Can You Trust the Mainstream Media?" by Andrew Harrison, Guardian News and Media Limited, August 6, 2017. Reprinted by permission.

If any piece of video can stand for the spirit of the times, then this fevered, resentful summer of 2017 could well be summed up in a clip of west London activist Ishmahil Blagrove, a film-maker and member of Justice4Grenfell, dispensing a furious dressing-down to a Sky reporter sent to cover the aftermath of London's most catastrophic fire in generations.

Blagrove seethes with righteous anger. "F--- the media, f--- the mainstream," he tells the TV journalist to cheers from passers-by, all the rage and frustration of the Grenfell disaster directed for a moment not at the borough council that enabled it but at those who covered it. Then he makes a connection familiar to old footsoldiers of the left and increasingly popular with its new recruits. Everything is connected. "For two years, you've hounded and demonised Jeremy Corbyn," Blagrove shouts. "You said he was unelectable. You created that narrative and people believed your bull---- for a while. But what this election has done is shown that people are immune. They're wearing bulletproof vests to you and the other billionaires of the media owners and Rupert Murdoch and all the m----------."

In years gone by, this might have been ignored as a standard everything-is-wrong jeremiad against the iniquities of the system. Blagrove is, after all, a veteran of Hyde Park's Speakers' Corner. But the clip went viral and clearly spoke to a wider audience. This summer, what was once a fringe analysis—that the media are not a complex collection of independent agencies holding the system to account but an elite-directed component of that system—finally moved into the popular consciousness.

After the bitter referendums over Scottish independence and Britain's EU membership, after newspapers and TV failed to predict the successes of Donald Trump, Brexit and Jeremy Corbyn, and finally with the nightmarish failure of policy and oversight that led to Grenfell, confidence in the media has taken a battering. And alternative voices are keen to undermine it further. From new, conspiracy-minded outlets such as the Canary and Evolve Politics to the "alt-right," libertarian and hard Brexit conversations that cluster on Twitter, the loudest and most strident voices push a relentless line: you can't trust the mainstream media.

It is not just the politically motivated who hold these beliefs. Judged on hard metrics, confidence in UK media has fallen noticeably in recent years. According to communications agency Edelman's 2017 Trust Barometer survey of 1,500 Britons, the number of people who said they trusted British news outlets at all fell from an already low 36% in 2015 to a mere 24% by the beginning of 2017. The 2017 *Digital News Report* from the Reuters Institute, published in June, found that just 41% of British people agreed that the news media did a good job in helping them distinguish fact from fiction. The figure for social media was even lower: 18%.

"It's a serious problem for the profession," says Dr Rasmus Kleis Nielsen of the Reuters Institute. "The political legitimacy of institutions like the BBC and also the business models of newspapers depend on the idea that they offer something trustworthy. Healthy distrust can be a good thing but hardened cynicism is paralysing."

He is worried that people are tending to judge the entire industry by its worst practitioners. "The danger is that the influential and the upper classes see journalism as too tabloid and populist, while working-class people think it pays little attention to people like themselves and their lives—and no one is happy."

"It is beginning to feel like a culture war," says Ian Katz, editor of BBC2's *Newsnight* and formerly deputy editor of the *Guardian*. The "attritional decline" in trust that he has witnessed during his 25 years in journalism has accelerated sharply over the past few years, he says. Now, when *Newsnight* sends reporters and producers to cover the Grenfell protests or June's van attack near Finsbury Park mosque, they are met with "extraordinary levels of hostility and suspicion."

"At Grenfell, a lot of the reaction crystallised around the idea of an establishment plot to minimise the extent of the catastrophe," Katz explains. "There was an elision of a whole series of things into the Grenfell disaster, including the perception that the media had failed to give Corbyn a fair crack. That hostility has become a proxy for wider, inchoate anger with the establishment in general and the press in particular."

He's talking about a new article of faith on the political left: that, in its attitudes to Corbyn, the media inadvertently revealed the truth about themselves. Instead of supporting Labour's new leader, goes the narrative, liberal newspapers such as the *Guardian* and *Observer*, along with "state broadcaster" the BBC, set out to destroy him. When Corbyn did better than expected in the 2017 general election, this proved that the media were unequivocally wrong and the Corbynites were right. Questions of a journalistic duty to examine, or the separation of news and comment, or even basing your coverage reasonably on the past performance of platforms similar to Corbyn's, were by the by. So was the point that Corbyn did not actually win the election. No matter—the liberal press had betrayed its readers and the MSM (mainstream media) had got it wrong.

"In terms of trust," says Kerry-Anne Mendoza, a founder of one of the most controversial of the new media outlets, the *Canary*, "how would you feel when a newspaper has always been critical of austerity and neoliberalism, but when a politician appears who actually stands against those things, those same liberal left papers call his supporters 'f---ing fools'?" She's using a single Nick Cohen column as a synecdoche for the entire liberal press, but it's central to the non-MSM worldview that the media be perceived as a consistent unit. "When it came down to it," she continues, "those liberal papers rallied to defend the system and that was appalling. That's where trust fell down. People stopped trusting their motives. And people like us decided they didn't want to put up with it any more."

Veteran media commentator Raymond Snoddy says: "What we've seen this year is that 'mainstream media' has changed from a general description into a term of abuse. We've seen trust in media ebb and flow over many years but there's been nothing like this before. There is now a completely different way of self-manufacturing and distributing news outside of the mainstream. These new outlets can be very diverse and exciting, but they exist outside any conventional sense of journalistic principles—of fact-checking and at least trying to get it objectively right."

Like any perfect storm, this one has taken time to gather. When the *News of the World* was revealed in 2011 to have targeted phone messages belonging to the murdered schoolgirl Milly Dowler, victims of the 7/7 bombings and many others, public revulsion was so overwhelming that it closed the paper. But recommendations for a new system of press control by the subsequent Leveson inquiry petered out and prosecutions connected to the scandal also proved anti-climactic. Though Rupert Murdoch experienced "the most humble day of my life" before the culture select committee in 2011, sections of the public felt that the press at large had got away with something, even if they couldn't say exactly what it was.

This discontent with the media began to coalesce as Britain entered its current period of political chaos. The Scottish independence referendum of 2014 saw the BBC attacked from the left as well as the right for a change, with legions of "cybernats" on social media casting the corporation as a Westminster mouthpiece and demonstrating outside BBC Scotland's Glasgow headquarters to demand the sacking of political editor, Nick Robinson.

"I don't think my offence was sufficient to justify 4,000 [most estimates said 1,000] people marching on the BBC's headquarters so that young men and women who are new to journalism have, like they do in Putin's Russia, to fight their way through crowds of protesters, frightened as to how they do their jobs," Robinson would tell an audience at the Edinburgh international book festival a year after the demonstration. "Alex Salmond was using me as a symbol of the wicked, metropolitan, Westminster classes sent from London in order to tell the Scots what they ought to do."

When Laura Kuenssberg took over from Robinson, the meme of the "Tory BBC" took hold and filtered into Corbynism. Kuenssberg became a lightning rod for the new left's dissatisfactions, the target of a petition demanding that she be sacked and for routine, vitriolic accusations of bias towards the government. Instances that did not fit the narrative, including Kuenssberg's frequent harsh questioning of Theresa May, were dismissed. For Conservatives used to their own adversarial relationship with the BBC, this was an unusual development.

"The current Labour leadership is used to being a backbench rebel movement, a protest movement," say Mark Wallace, editor of ConservativeHome. "The scrutiny you face when pitching to run the country is of a different order and that's proving uncomfortable for them. I think there's a knowing element to the endless personal pursuit of Laura Kuenssberg as well. If you bombard someone for long enough, they might never actually surrender to you, but it may have a chilling effect on what questions they ask."

Wallace doesn't know a single Conservative MP or minister who feels they get an easy ride from Kuenssberg. "Politicians understand that they operate in a risky environment. They know that journalists can enhance their careers by asking tough questions and catching politicians out. That's how it should be."

In parallel with Corbynism, the EU referendum campaign and its aftermath had their own corrosive effect on trust in the media. In the press, the line between campaigning and reporting dissolved as rightwing titles threw themselves wholeheartedly behind Leave. TV coverage became a battleground. Leave campaigners claimed to have identified consistent pro-EU bias from the BBC. Remainers detected dangerous instances of false balance, most notoriously when a poll found that 88% of UK economists were against Brexit, only for their views to be set repeatedly against those of a single economist, Professor Patrick Minford, who said that Brexit would not damage trade and the UK economy. This and other coverage distorted the vote, say Remainers, by creating a misleading impression that experts were split on the issue.

"Economic and political truth isn't discovered by a straw poll," argues Wallace, a Leave supporter. "If one person's right and everyone else is wrong, that single person is still right. I actually think the BBC made great efforts to be balanced during the referendum. The Ukip surge and the feedback they got showed that Euroscepticism was more popular than they'd thought."

When the BBC says that it is criticised from both sides and so it must be doing something right, Wallace thinks it has a point. "There's also the more reasoned critique, which is the unconscious bias that comes when you recruit people who look and sound like you and were educated in similar places to you," he says. "The traditional flaws we see in the BBC might not come from intentional bias but an assumption that they are the sensible centre-ground, so how could anyone possibly disagree with them?"

As the Brexit dust settled, a King's College London investigation, "UK media coverage of the 2016 EU referendum campaign," concluded that "the implications of a divisive, antagonistic and hyper-partisan campaign—by the campaigners themselves as much as by many national media outlets—is likely to shape British politics for the foreseeable future." In other words, Brexit poisoned the well of trust still further.

Across the Atlantic, the success of Donald Trump's post-truth platform, where every criticism was dismissed as a politicised attack and all media but the most slavish were failing and lying, introduced the concept of "fake news" as a way to discredit and disempower the inconvenient mainstream media. Toxic to the American body politic, fake news is actually a rarity in Britain. "People who talk about fake news in the UK are guilty of fake news themselves," argues Dominic Ponsford, editor of *Press Gazette*. "Manufacturing stories to further a political aim or to make money through clicks just doesn't happen in the UK.

"What we do have is highly partisan news and coverage when it comes in our national press. What's changed is that the *Sun* or the *Mail* are now amplified by social media to people who don't necessarily read those papers."

In other words, social media is showing us what always went on in the papers we never read—and convincing us that the press is getting worse and worse.

But if a British reader's Facebook feed isn't as full of fictional, manipulative stories as their American counterpart's, the suspicion of fake news is still out there, degrading trust in what you see and read. "Fake news is a double-edged sword and a worrying concept," says Nielsen. "It allows established media like the *New York Times* or the *Guardian* to market itself as an antidote to deliberate untruth. But the problem is that talking about fake news obscures the more dangerous story—which is that much of the public has very low confidence in the 'non-fake' work of professional journalists."

All these threads of suspicion and system failure came together in the horror of Grenfell, which brought its own bad news for supporters of traditional media. If Brexit, Trump and Corbyn were failures of national media then this was a failure of local journalism—to investigate municipal mismanagement and prevent such disasters from happening in the first place. "The local press has experienced a devastating collapse over the last decade," says Ponsford. "There are whole boroughs of London that don't have any journalists covering them at all. Kensington and Chelsea would have had a dozen journalists based in that borough 25 years ago. There's no one there now. That can only mean that the councils there are not being scrutinised."

"The best journalism happens at a local level, there's no doubt about it," says Ted Jeory, whose Trial By Jeory blog and column in the *East London Advertiser* exposed the Tower Hamlets corruption scandal that saw Lutfur Rahman removed as mayor and banned from standing for office. "But morale is very poor and there's a cultural shift in national papers at news editor level. You used to start on a local paper, learn how to knock on doors and be tenacious. Now, people are being recruited at national level and sometimes becoming news editors without having done any of that local stuff."

The collapse of the local press also has ramifications for who work in journalism and how they approach the job. The path from local paper to national newsroom was once a viable career route for bright, working-class people who might not have been to university, but today a young journalist might enter the industry on a national paper's website. And, says Ponsford, they might not leave the office at all in the course of a hard day's Googling and content aggregation.

The need for a degree and the family wherewithal to survive in London on minimal wages mean that the diversity of the media pool, mostly based in the capital, suffers further. Working-class and minority candidates find it harder to get in. A 2016 survey by City University indicated that only 0.4% of working journalists are Muslim and only 0.2% are black, when almost 5% of the UK population is Muslim and 3% is black. A Sutton Trust survey the same year found that 54% of senior print journalists attended Oxford or Cambridge and 51% went to private school.

"It's plainly the case that shows like ours could benefit from a greater degree of diversity," says Katz, "not just ethnic diversity but of background, class and education. It's a criticism that hurts because it's got some truth to it." Viewers need to see people on TV who look and sound like them if they're going to be confident in what they hear. Katz describes an endless battle to ensure that *Newsnight* discussion panels are not solely composed of middle-aged white males. "If you were in here, you would see us with our heads in our hands looking at the guest list going, 'This is ridiculous.'"

Some are less sure that belief in established media is in such steep decline. Emily Bell is a former editor of the *Guardian* website and now director of the Tow Center for Digital Journalism at Columbia University, New York. "We should be careful about exactly who is telling us that mainstream media is less trusted and why that narrative is circulated," she says. "It's often politicians like Trump or new media outlets seeking to establish their own credibility or propagandists or PR companies. It's people with a vested interest. That doesn't mean the media isn't having problems. But is trust really declining or are we just being told that it is?"

She points out that less ideologically motivated audiences—"if you're not a Corbynista or a Ukipper or a Trump supporter or a brocialist [a male socialist or progressive who downplays women's issues], for instance"—are consuming mainstream media in greater quantities. In America, CNN is having a "spectacular" year in terms of viewing figures and advertising. "You might see a broken business model but you're not seeing a diminution of consumption like you would if something was really becoming irrelevant or discredited."

While Trump and the conspiracist alternative media push the narrative of fake news, the press has seen improvement on one of the most stringent measures of trust: would you give this organisation money? One executive at the *Washington Post* told Bell: "It's fantastic. Every time Trump criticises us there's a spike in subscriptions."

"The more that media outlets multiply," she says, "the more the phrase 'the media' becomes meaningless." If you're under 25, then BuzzFeed is possibly more representative of mainstream media than ITV and the *Daily Telegraph*, whose output you never consume. Do you trust Buzzfeed because it's more accurate or because it conforms to your preferences? Bell thinks the focus on trust rather than quality is misplaced. "People trusted the media more when you only had the six o'clock news and Walter Cronkite, but I don't think there's any evidence that news coverage before 1975 was inherently more accurate or comprehensive than the best journalism today. In many ways it's better now.

"No literate society should aim for 100% trust in its media. You want a reasonable scepticism without total cynicism. What you want," she says, "is for people to question."

Which is exactly what Kerry-Anne Mendoza would say the *Canary* does. Founded in 2015 with the aim of disrupting a predominantly conservative media landscape, the site has become one of the most shared and notorious of the new left news outlets. "Journalists should agitate against corporate or political power or the power of the wealthy, or frankly the power of the media, to produce balanced opinions," says Mendoza. "I think it's the central role of the press."

Yet the success of the *Canary* is attributable less to conventional campaigning journalism and more to hyper-partisan coverage designed to confirm its readers' prejudices. Describing itself as "fresh, fearless, independent journalism," the *Canary* delivers a daily diet of vociferously pro-Corbyn, anti-establishment stories where news and editorial comment are indistinguishable. Its method of paying contributors is what sets its overheated tone: writers are paid a share of advertising revenue proportionate to the traffic that their news story generates, on top of a flat fee drawn from readers' voluntary subscription payments. It is an innovative revenue share that has enabled several *Canary* writers to make a career from journalism. But it can only encourage them to seek maximum clicks via the most lurid headlines and to put the most alarming construction on the flimsiest evidence.

In *Canary*-world, an off-the-cuff comment by an unnamed Tory MP at an EU referendum party ("Who the f--- cares if sterling's falling? You'll be all right; I'll be all right. It's a revolution!") becomes "The horrific, drunken response from a potential Tory leader after he realised Brexit will crush ordinary families." Video of a police stop and search becomes "Watch six police officers humiliate a Muslim woman for wearing a headscarf." And the decision of a constituency Labour party to send one not two delegates to the party conference becomes "Labour elites just crushed party democracy to ensure they choose Jeremy Corbyn's successor." Common themes are the persecution of Corbyn and the refusal of the mainstream media to talk about the stories that the *Canary* has uncovered. And its readers love it.

"All credit to the *Canary* for what they've achieved," says Ponsford, "but I am alarmed when people hold them up as a paragon. A lot of it is good sensational political reporting but some stuff appears there which you'd never expect to see on any professional website. Some of the stories they run are plain bats--t."

Understandably, Mendoza vigorously defends her site's editorial approach. "We felt the left had lost the power to tell stories," she says. "If you're going to have a conversation that's big enough to change the country, then you have to speak to all of the people in a language that's going to connect with them." She is, in her way, an idealist.

But when I put it to her that the *Canary* has built its business by creating the most emotive stories often on the back of very little evidence, she makes an astonishing claim: "If a story is hyperbole, then often it won't get shared on the progressive side of the debate. That sort of thing is more popular on the political right."

This, in my experience, is flatly untrue. The MSM-doubting new left is absolutely addicted to overwrought stories, grain of truth or none. "If you over-promise and under-deliver enough," Mendoza continues, "the readers will just walk away." The success of certain *Canary* stories suggest that the opposite is true.

I ask her about some of the *Canary*'s most controversial items and whether it was responsible to publish them. In June 2016, the *Canary* ran a story headlined: "The truth behind the Labour coup, when it really began and who manufactured it (EXCLUSIVE)." It claimed that the leadership challenge against Corbyn was organised by the Fabian Society and a PR company called Portland Communications, "a company organised, fronted and controlled by a plethora of apparatchiks of Tony Blair and the centre-right of Labour."

Far from establishing a conspiracy, the story merely set out a series of unsurprising relationships between former senior employees of the Blair and Brown governments who had moved into lobbying. It added the names of a few betes-noirs of the left (Peter Mandelson, Alastair Campbell) and asserted in slippery language that the "coup" "appears to have been orchestrated" by the Fabians and Portland. There were no memos and no evidence of meetings, strategy or instructions for this scheme, only dark innuendo.

Nevertheless, the story spread across social media. Unite general secretary, Len McCluskey, gave it credence on *The Andrew Marr Show* and one Portland employee received a death threat.

Was it right for the *Canary* to create such a provocative story with so little basis in fact?

"I'm not willing to discuss it," is Mendoza's reply. "We put it to bed well over a year ago. That was an awful smear campaign against us and I don't want to add anything further to it. It's over."

But it isn't. There was no retraction and the Portland conspiracy still crops up in Labour forums.

I turn to another questionable *Canary* story: "A major media outlet just revealed who won the US election … a week in advance." This item claimed that a TV station called WCRB had somehow inadvertently published the predetermined results of the November 2016 American presidential election. Wasn't this story, based on a mere dummy graphic used for rehearsal purposes, inflammatory nonsense?

"Yes, it was untrue and we issued a correction," Mendoza replies. "But let me ask you: how many corrections has the *Observer* published in the last few months? We are human beings and we make mistakes. Did we clean up the mess and make sure it's clear to our readership? Yes we did and that's what is important to us."

I check the page after our conversation ends. The story is still up on the site, the only apparent correction a statement from WCRB, confirming that the graphic was indeed meaningless test data. Otherwise, its baseless speculation remains intact and live on the internet.

Mendoza is right. People do make mistakes. But a mainstream media site would remove every trace of a false story like this. *Observer* readers' editor, Stephen Pritchard, said: "Kerry-Anne Mendoza appears not to be aware that the paper publishes corrections every week and has done for more than 16 years. These also appear online. Many more smaller corrections are made to web stories, each one carefully footnoted so the reader is in no doubt what changes have been made and when. It's all part of a serious attempt to be open, transparent and accountable."

If one story exemplifies how news and information move in the world of alternative news it is the tale of the Grenfell D notice.

THE MOST TRUSTED NEWS ORGANIZATION?

Our recent report, Political Polarization and Media Habits, finds that trust and distrust in the news media varies greatly by political ideology. Many readers asked us: Among the 36 news organizations we asked about, which one do Americans trust most? The answer is more complex than it may seem and can be measured in a number of different ways. Here's a breakdown:

1. The full population picture doesn't tell the whole story. If you look simply at the total percentage of online adults who say they trust a news organization for news about government and politics, several mainstream television outlets rise to the top. CNN, ABC, NBC, CBS and Fox News are all trusted by more than four-in-ten web-using US adults. These high numbers, though, are intertwined with the fact that more than nine-in-ten respondents have heard of these five news sources. Trust and distrust were only asked of sources respondents had heard of, thus, the better known a source is, the more Americans in total who can voice trust or distrust of that source.

2. Is a news organization not trusted? Or just not well known? An alternative way to analyze the data is to look at the percent of trust among those who have heard of the news organization. This approach means that lesser-known outlets may be seen as equally trusted as better-known outlets. By this metric, several of the best-known sources sit toward the top, joined by some less familiar sources. NPR, for example, is on par with many of the mainstream television outlets on this measure. Among the panelists who have heard of NPR, 55% trust it. The same is true of 57% of those who have heard of CNN and 53% of those who have heard of NBC and of ABC.

3. What about the ratio of trust to distrust? Another way to think of trust is to compare trust and distrust in a news source. In other words, what is the ratio of people who trust a news outlet to those who distrust it? This ratio is based just on those who have rated the sources as trusted or distrusted, regardless of how well known the source is.

The result is a different list of news brands: the *Economist*, BBC, NPR, PBS and the *Wall Street Journal* are among those with the highest ratio of trust to distrust.

"Which News Organization Is the Most Trusted? The Answer Is Complicated,"
by Amy Mitchell, Pew Research Center, October 30, 2014.

On 16 June, two days after the fatal fire, leftwing blog Skwawkbox wrote "multiple sources" had told them that "the government has placed a 'D notice' ... on the real number of deaths in the blaze." The blog repeated claims that unnamed firefighters had seen up to 200 bodies in the ruins of Grenfell, far more than the official total so far of 30 dead (police now estimate there were 80 deaths in the block).

The story had everything: government conspiracy, evasion and callousness plus a wall of silence from traditional media. It duly received uncountable shares and furious denunciation across multiple Twitter and Facebook accounts. The only problem was it wasn't true.

"Any professional journalist could tell you that this story didn't remotely hold up," says City University journalism professor George Brock, himself once a member of the D notice committee. "The D notice system is a voluntary one and it is inconceivable that any government would try to use it for this purpose. If they were foolish enough to try, it would be about 20 seconds before the story got out."

Yet weeks after the story was debunked in a forensic takedown by BuzzFeed's James Ball, and after Skwawkbox published a highly qualified "update," again with the original false story intact, it was still being shared on social media as fact.

I speak on the phone to Steve Walker, the self-employed Merseyside businessman who runs Skwawkbox. For someone only recently unmasked and monstered by the Mail Online ("it's a bit of a badge of honour"), he's surprisingly amiable towards a journalist he's never met.

Walker launched Skwawkbox in 2012 to write about the NHS, the welfare system and the state of the left, then found new impetus with the advent of Corbyn. "The people we're trying to reach are what we call the outer parts of the Venn diagram," he says. "Not the real dedicated people on the left, but maybe their auntie or their uncle who reads their Facebook page. With the right story, they'll share it and spread the word."

How could it have been right for Skwawkbox to spread unsubstantiated rumour at a time when riots were considered a genuine possibility? Walker's response is that the story was caveated with multiple "sources say" and "reports have been received," a defence that wouldn't pass muster in elementary journalism school. "At no point did I say, 'This is true,'" he argues. "That would be me spreading fake news if it turned out to be untrue." But that's exactly what Skwawkbox did. No reputable newspaper would "correct" a false story merely by placing an update at the top of the page, leaving the false story intact below and, by implication, still valid.

"Frankly, I don't take any responsibility for people who can't read the qualifications or choose not to," Walker answers. "My obligation is more to the people out there rather than what the journalistic establishment considers the usual way of doing things. That story went viral because people said, why is nobody talking about what we are seeing on the ground? There's already far too much suppression out there. People deserve the chance to make their own mind up.

"And," he adds, "I'm still not convinced by the denials."

Which raises the question: how can you make up your mind when your information sources are so polluted by fiction that even the people who spread them believe them? The response of self-defined insurgent media is: why observe the rules of the mainstream media when the mainstream media have failed us? If the authorities deny a story, well they would, wouldn't they?

For professional journalists, this is a nightmare prospect: news and commentary devolving into a baseless cacophony where anyone can say anything and whatever is shared most will win. The truth will become what the most, or the loudest, people want it to be.

And yet, for all the chaos and uncertainty in the media, it's worth remembering that we've been here before, albeit a long time ago. In the 1820s, the written press in Britain had become so elitist, complacent and deferential that dissenting journalists launched papers known as the "unstamped" because they refused to pay the newspaper tax. "My God, they were violently opinionated," says Brock. "They made the *Canary* and Skwawkbox look restrained."

Similarly, in the United States in the 60s, the cultural and political crisis of Vietnam brought on a slump in the credibility of a similarly stuffy and obeisant mass media. The journalism of the 1970s proved to have rather sharper teeth. Just ask Richard Nixon.

"What I'm saying is, mistrust in journalism is not an unambiguous disaster," Brock continues. "It may lead readers and journalists to think more critically. I deplore it when alternative media present themselves as news channels when in fact they're highly activist blogs with strong but narrow points of view. But they exist, and when you're faced with something you can't uninvent, you have to learn from it.

"In the last analysis," says Brock, "professional mainstream journalists can always say, we've checked this out and it stands up."

It's an answer I hear from many professional journalists I talk to. The answer to bad journalism can only be good journalism, from the widest pool of professionals. Fund and deliver it in the most innovative ways you can, but let the material be its own advocate. It's all you can do.

"The people who want to see journalism fail now have a bigger megaphone than ever," says Bell. "But the good news is that the world is getting more complicated, so it needs good journalism."

The mainstream media's job is to remind the audiences of tomorrow of that fact. Trust isn't given. It's earned. And if there's one basic truth that every storyteller understands, it's that if you want to be believed, don't tell—show.

Periodical and Internet Sources Bibliography

The following articles have been selected to supplement the diverse views presented in this chapter.

"America Might See a New Constitutional Convention in a Few Years," The Economist, September 30, 2017. https://www .economist.com/briefing/2017/09/30/america-might-see-a-new-constitutional-convention-in-a-few-years.

Janna Anderson and Lee Rainie, "The future of truth and misinformation online," Pew Internet, October 19, 2017. http:// www.pewinternet.org/2017/10/19/the-future-of-truth-and-misinformation-online/.

"How to detect bias in news media," Fair.org, https://fair.org/take-action-now/media-activism-kit/how-to-detect-bias-in-news-media/.

James Fallows, "'There's No Such Thing Anymore, Unfortunately, as Facts,'" The Atlantic, November 30, 2016. https://www .theatlantic.com/notes/2016/11/theres-no-such-thing-any-more-unfortunately-as-facts/509276/.

Natalie Fenton, "Journalism and democracy: Towards a comprehensive research strategy in Mexico," Goldsmiths University of London, https://freedomhouse.org/sites/default/files/Journalism%20and%20Democracy_Towards%20a.

Maria Popova, "Lying in politics: Hannah Arendt on deception, self-deception, and the psychology of defactualization," BrainPickings. June 15, 2016. https://www.brainpickings .org/2016/06/15/lying-in-politics-hannah-arendt/%20 contemporary%20research%20strategy%20in%20Mexico.pdf.

Molly Worthen, "The Evangelical Roots of Our Post-Truth Society," The New York Times, April 13, 2017. https://www.nytimes .com/2017/04/13/opinion/sunday/the-evangelical-roots-of-our-post-truth-society.html.

Bob Weeks, "Arguments for and against term limits," Wichita Liberty, May 30, 2014. https://wichitaliberty.org/politics/arguments-term-limits/.

How Secure Is the Politician-Media Marriage?

Chapter Preface

Anyone who followed the relationship between President Donald Trump and the media understood that he forged his own path. He sought to control the message and allow the messenger to run wild. Frequent press briefings provided him the opportunity to leak out whatever information or misinformation he preferred. Presidential press conferences became frighteningly rare and talks to the nation gave no chance for questioning and only a post-game rebuttal by a Democratic representative.

Whether the Trump approach is the reckoning of a new and permanent state of reality in the relationship between the president and media remains to be seen, but it is likely that future White House residents will be more open to conversations with the press. Trump is an anomaly who plays to the fears of biases of many of his constituents by complaining that the media is slanted with a vendetta against him and them. To remedy that, he took to Twitter to get his message across without being forced to engage in direct debate.

Trump is not alone among politicians in his mistrust of the media. Social media has allowed many to divorce themselves from any one-on-one conflict with reporters and control the dialogue. Journalists are often treated with disdain and condescension.

Times have indeed changed since the advent of the Internet and cable television. The sheer number of outlets that cannot be considered unbiased give politicians opportunities to choose which to support with appearances and interviews. For instance, those on the right are likely to be seen on Fox News and those on the left appear on MSNBC. Many believe that the explosion of so-called news sources that barely hide their agendas on the Internet, cable, and social media has weakened American journalism and created an environment in which politicians are free to lie without retribution.

"Greater control of the news by those who work in covering the news can't be separated from the larger goal of greater control by all workers over their working conditions."

American Journalism Is Failing Democracy

Robert Jensen

In the following viewpoint Robert Jensen takes a hypercritical look at the current state of the news media. He offers that American news outlets are more driven by profit and increasing ratings through entertainment than embracing their intended jobs of disseminating the news in an unbiased manner. The author argues that a general contributing problem is the weakening of the labor union in America that places too much power at those at the top, who are driven more by economic gain than truth-telling. Robert Jensen is a professor in the journalism department of the University of Texas at Austin.

"American Journalism Is Failing Democracy," by Robert Jensen, The President and Fellows of Harvard College. Published by arrangement with the Nieman foundation for Journalism. Reprinted by permission.

As you read, consider the following questions:

1. How does the author tie the struggles of labor in the United States with changes in media behavior?
2. What is the author's opinion of the contentions in the book he refers to in the following article?
3. Does the author successfully argue that American journalism is indeed failing democracy?

My heart is with Arthur Rowse's critique of contemporary journalism. As a former journeyman newspaper reporter and editor who still writes frequently for popular audiences, I too feel betrayed by an American news media that is increasingly cowed by concentrated economic power and complicit with elites in the slow but unmistakable decay of real democracy.

Rowse offers a clear and compelling account of the symptoms of the news media's failures in *Drive-By Journalism*, but in the end I think his diagnosis of the causes of the problems misses the mark, which sends his prescriptions veering off target. In short: Mainstream commercial journalism is in as sorry shape as Rowse contends, but not exactly for the reasons he assumes, and it can't be fixed in the ways he suggests. Rowse describes the disturbing trends in journalism, in regard both to what is and isn't covered in the news, and tells important stories about journalists asleep at the switch. But I think a more radical analysis is needed to guide reform.

From the first pages of the book, Rowse doesn't hold back on his critique: "Rather than using its freedom to foster the informed citizenry necessary for a vital democracy, the press has been merging competing voices into a homogenized newsamuse cartel. It exploits the First Amendment for commercial gain, shaping politics to its own needs, allowing advertisers and publicity agents to color the news and destroying public servants with cheap, shallow 'gotcha' journalism, the bastard child of informed investigative reporting." The book details the "self-censorship, predatory practices, commercial pressures and political bias" that Rowse says have plagued the press for years. Today, "the detrimental forces are stronger and the consequences more serious," he warns.

Rowse's impressive résumé includes stints at the *Boston Globe*, the *Washington Post*, and *U.S. News & World Report*, along with books and numerous freelance articles (including for *Nieman Reports*). He comes to the task with an obvious love of the craft nurtured through long experience in the business. This is both a strength of the book and a limitation. On the plus side: Rowse seems to have seen firsthand, or reported on, virtually every type of journalistic malfeasance, and he writes in a fierce and lean style infused with a passion for politics and the press. On the negative: He overestimates the influence of the media.

The book is at its best when it goes after the hypocrisy of the news business, such as in the chapter "Exploiting the First Amendment for Profit." Rowse details the shameful behavior of greedy and self-interested media corporations on such issues as telecommunications legislation, and he rightly charges the industry with helping redefine the First Amendment to protect corporate rights. The result, he says, is a process by which "citizen democracy is being replaced by corporate democracy."

Another of my favorite chapters is about public relations. Here he shows how managers' pressure on news organizations to save money makes the manipulation of journalists easier than ever for politicians' publicists and the propaganda machine of corporations. This happens not only through the usual p.r. mechanisms but also through the creation of phony "citizens groups" funded by the business community.

Despite all that I like about the way Rowse tells the story, I think his analysis is too media-centric, both in assessing blame for the country's political situation and in looking for solutions. In Rowse's view, "Controlling what people see and hear is the ultimate power." There's a way in which that is true, of course; if people aren't allowed to know certain things, it's hard for them to know how to act. People with power in the United States long ago

WANTED: MEDIA WATCHDOG

Last week the media came unglued when Trump Administration staffers excluded major news outlets from a White House press briefing. Institutions like the *LA Times*, the *New York Times*, Politico and CNN were not invited to take part in the briefing.

President Trump himself has been an outspoken critic of the news institutions and the action of denying them access was no doubt a power tactic to remind them that he is in control.

His criticism of publications, networks and individual reporters have long been a part of his persona, but now that he is president, it's more than a little tawdry.

I've written before about his unfortunate use of his platform at a CIA memorial event to rail against media outlets who criticize him. I've shared my thoughts about how he emasculated CNN during a recent press conference by labeling them a "fake news" outlet.

Don't get me wrong—after years of mainstream media malpractice, was it strangely satisfying? Absolutely.

Both liberal and conservative leaning organizations are responsible for losing their own moral authority to claim objectivity or trust when they've given pass after pass to prior administrations and scandals.

One of the biggest issues I have is when journalism entities preach objectivity but produce consistently slanted stories to praise or criticize a subject they may or may not like.

learned that controlling the public mind is in many ways a more efficient form of social control than the violence that totalitarian systems use to control people's behavior directly.

But in our system this doesn't mean that ultimate control over the picture of the world presented in mass media rests with news organizations, let alone with journalists. Rowse argues that, "When it comes to running the country, there's no power higher than media power." Yes, media influence is powerful. But real power lies in the institutions that control resources and decision-making, and media corporations are but one segment of that power, not the ultimate power.

Leave the personal thoughts and opinion to the editorial department. That's their job.

Added to the mix, unfortunately, is that all too often news consumers have a hard time understanding what is news and what is opinion.

A great example of this is the primetime lineup on Fox News or MSNBC. Nearly all of the programming during that time frame consists of opinion shows hosted by commentators, not journalists. But throughout the rest of the broadcast day, the programs are dedicated to news, hosted by journalists and reporters.

Do they bring in guests with perspectives? Yes, to offer opposing viewpoints or to spark a debate amongst guests on the issue.

Journalism has a mix of both reporting and perspective, most of which is reasoned and respectful.

Journalism is also imperfect. Should media outlets do everything possible to curb errors? Of course.

Some are better than others at holding strong internal standards, but it is up to the news consumer to hold their media accountable—it should never be up to a politician, right or left.

"Wade Heath: Media Should Be Held Accountable, Not Silenced," by Wade Heath, Lodinews.com, March 1, 2017.

This means that Rowse's prescription for improving the health of our political system primarily through media reform misses the point. Media reform is crucial, but it has to be part of a larger social movement that addresses illegitimate structures of authority and unjust concentrations of power throughout the society, in private and public arenas. In other words, a revitalization of progressive politics more broadly is necessary. But Rowse dismisses such hope for "sweeping changes in American politics" as a "pipe dream" and says we have a better chance of "changing media practices than political views."

I don't know of anyone concerned with the decay of democracy who doesn't understand the importance of mass media, but media reform cannot happen in a political vacuum. For example, one of Rowse's suggestions is "to seek broad agreement with Wall Street to allow media managers to remove news operations from the same profit goals imposed on other divisions and lower short-term profit goals in order to preserve long-term profitability and foster more responsible journalism." But why would Wall Street respond to such a plea? If investors thought it was in their interests to pursue responsible journalism because it was more profitable, they would. But for the most part they don't, and there's nothing in the structure of corporate capitalism to motivate them to change.

Rowse offers the beginnings of a radical analysis but doesn't head in the radical direction necessary. That illustrates another aspect of the problem with mainstream contemporary journalism— the way in which journalists reflexively operate within the narrow ideological framework of American politics. The visible political spectrum in the United States, which has always been far less expansive than in most of the rest of the world, runs from the hard right to the liberal. While all shades of reactionary ideas are routinely aired in the United States, very little of left/progressive/ radical thinking is allowed in the mainstream. For an example, just look at how hard politicians of both major parties and journalists worked to keep Ralph Nader out of the 2000 presidential contest.

Rowse positions himself at the critical edge of that visible spectrum, but he is unwilling to step very far outside it. The reason for stressing this about a book that I think generally is on target is not to engage in a who-can-be-more-critical contest but to be clear about the assumptions that underlie our analyses so that we are clear about where we are heading. Like Rowse, I believe that serious media reform is essential. But that project should go forward yoked to a strengthening of labor rights, curbs on corporate power, and a host of other progressive political projects. For example, decision-making authority over the news should be transferred from corporate managers to working journalists, but that kind of change isn't going to happen without a revitalization of the US labor movement. Greater control of the news by those who work in covering the news can't be separated from the larger goal of greater control by all workers over their working conditions.

At the core of all of these struggles has to be a rejection of the key ideological dogmas of the culture—that "free" markets in contemporary capitalism are a vehicle for democracy and that the United States is a benevolent force for peace in the world— accompanied by a willingness to ask tough questions and find honest answers. Journalists have a role in these struggles, maybe even a special role. But to place too much hope in journalism is both unfair to journalists and unwise for us all.

> *"Saying every journalist should
> have no bias is kind of like saying
> everyone should be expected to love
> every single aspect of their job. …
> Just because I personally hate a
> certain politician or a certain law,
> that does not mean I cannot cover
> the topic in an unbiased fashion."*

Bias Is Natural for Journalists

Thor Benson

*In the following viewpoint Thor Benson argues that natural biases
based on opinions of journalists should not have an impact on the
truthfulness in the industry itself. He offers that media members can
divorce themselves of their personal views while reporting without
slant. While that is certainly the case, others might argue that many
simply do allow their own prejudices to enter into their reporting.
That is nothing new—such has been the case since journalism
began. But the sheer number of news outlets in the modern era
allow biased reporting to flourish. Thor Benson is a journalist whose
work has been featured in the* Atlantic, Slate, *the* New Republic,
and other publications.

"Every Journalist Is Biased and That's Fine," by Thor Benson, Paste Media Group, May 2, 2017. Reprinted by permission.

As you read, consider the following questions:

1. Does the author believe that slanted reporting is not a problem for American journalism?
2. How does the author separate the notion of unbiased reporting from the obligation to criticize in regard to President Trump?
3. Why does the author believe bias in a journalist can be a positive?

I am a journalist, and I have been called biased many times. When a stranger on the internet calls me this, it seems they believe that I will become overwhelmed with anxiety and jump at the chance to display my indifference. That is not what happens. I am biased, and so are all journalists, and that's perfectly fine.

To say you are completely unbiased would be to say you are not human. Humans are creatures with opinions, and even if you don't care about a topic that much, you always come to it with some preconceived notions and stances. The fact of the matter is that almost no journalist covers a topic they have no interest in, so it is much more likely they will have many opinions and strong feelings about whatever they cover. Any journalist who tells you they are unbiased should not be trusted or listened to, because they're either lying or ignorant.

Saying every journalist should have no bias is kind of like saying everyone should be expected to love every single aspect of their job. It's like saying if you don't love every aspect of your job, then you are incapable of doing your job. This is obviously false. Just because I personally hate a certain politician or a certain law, that does not mean I cannot cover the topic in an unbiased fashion.

There have been countless times I've forced myself to include information about something I despise that makes the subject look better than I'd personally like to make them look. I have written about how a politician lied about something but then also included that the lie really isn't that big of a deal for various reasons, for example. If my bias prevented me from including this information, then you could say there is a problem, but that is not the case. I believe it is not the case with most journalists, based on my experience.

There is a big difference between what a journalist wants to say based on their opinions and what ends up in an article. If a journalist is writing an opinion piece, then of course it will mostly include one side of the issue at hand, but they'll typically be far more even-handed when they're writing a report. Despite these seemingly obvious truths, I still constantly see journalists trying to pretend they're not biased to save face.

I have seen multiple articles from the hyper-conservative website and magazine *National Review* lamenting bias in the media. I always laugh when I see these articles, because some of the explicit bias I've seen in *National Review* articles could be spotted by the most casual reader. However, in the spirit of fairness and presenting multiple sides, I'll point out that opinion writer Jonah Goldberg wrote a decent op-ed for the *National Review* about media bias at the end of last year.

In the piece, Goldberg explains that most journalists are going to be biased, and they should simply be forthcoming about their bias. When this happens, people can be aware of it and decide if it has impacted their writing. "None of this means liberals—or conservatives—can't be good reporters, but the idea that media bias is nonexistent is ludicrous," he wrote. Goldberg is correct in this statement. Liberals and conservatives can be biased and good at their jobs, and personal bias is everywhere.

There was also a pervasive idea that presented itself throughout the campaign and since Donald Trump took office: the media is too hard on him. As a journalist, I feel qualified to explain the most important goal of journalism, which I think is to inform the public of dangers. There's a reason the news covers crime, natural disasters and more. When a politician poses a unique risk to the safety of Americans, it is the job of the press to illuminate what the dangers are. If Trump is scapegoating Muslims and immigrants to gain power, which may put those groups in danger, the press is right to be critical of this. If he has a temperament that might lead us into an international disaster, that's important to point out.

Furthermore, many of the people who think the press is too critical of Trump think the press was too easy on President Obama and too comfy with Hillary Clinton—despite the fact Clinton's email problems and other flaws dominated many news cycles. This is an odd sort of cognitive dissonance that I have trouble understanding. Would it be preferable if the press went easy on Trump because you believe they were allegedly easy on Obama? I don't think so. If the press was too easy on Obama, which is certainly debatable, the fact they're now being the check on presidential power they're always supposed to be is not a negative thing. It could actually be considered sort of refreshing.

Finally, it's important to note that having some opinionated journalists out there can be rewarding for readers and other journalists. I know that there are certain writers out there I typically agree with like Glenn Greenwald and Matt Taibbi. Knowing where they stand and what they believe in is personally very enjoyable for me, because it means I know who to go to when I'm first approaching a new topic that I think I'm going to care about. I can read what they said, which I know is coming from a perspective that is similar to my own, and I can use it as a starting point for figuring out what I think of the issue. Sometimes I disagree with their perspectives, but I at least get where they're coming from. From there I can go to other sources.

This is all to say that we will never kill bias in journalism, and there's nothing wrong with that. It's always going to be there, and sometimes it's actually a good thing. Does it annoy me when hacks at Infowars try to portray themselves as real journalists? Of course (and they're not), but that's not the main issue here. The main issue is that your average conservative or liberal journalist can do their jobs adequately if they're working under decent editors and truly care about journalism.

> *"The way we cover politics serves nobody well. Turnout at elections goes down. Do ordinary people enjoy the soundbites and the snarling? No. Look at how daily newspaper sales flattened in June through all the euro posturing."*

Politics and Media Are Changing

Sunder Katwala, Ben Whitford, and Carlos Ottery

In the following viewpoint Sunder Katwala, Ben Whitford and Carlos Ottery curate the words of experts, which indicate that criticism of the media in Great Britain has taken on a far different form than it has in the United States. Many in that country believe that media criticism of the government has been too harsh and that journalists must allow politicians to do their jobs, if not unfettered, at least without such a high level of condemnation. This all-encompassing piece seeks out views from various angles. Katwala is director of British Future and former general secretary of the Fabian Society. Whitford is a freelance journalist who writes for the Guardian, Newsweek *and* Slate. *Ottery is on staff at the* Guardian.

"Politics and the Media: Is It Time for Change?" by Sunder Katwala, Ben Whitford and Carlos Ottery, Guardian News and Media Limited, July 27, 2003. Reprinted by permission.

As you read, consider the following questions:

1. Are there wide-ranging opinions posted here about the state of British journalism or do most offer similar takes?
2. Based on this article, how does criticism about the media in Great Britain differ from that in the United States?
3. Does this article strongly indicate that the government has been treated too harshly by British journalists?

M ust relations between politicians and the press involve spin and fury? Does our macho media and political culture turn off voters or should we be proud of it? How could things be different? We ask the experts . . .

"There are problems on both sides. Tabloid values belong neither in Downing Street nor broadcasting. But politicians and their staff will use whatever means they have to defend themselves in a tight corner.

"So we do need a robust, confident media. We should all try to sober up after Dr Kelly's death. We ought to try to re-establish a viable working relationship. The Government ought to be willing to be held to account by the media as a matter of right, not of favour and spin.

"In return, as such papers as the *Observer* and *Guardian* have tried to do, we ought to be clear about our responsibilities and admit our mistakes."

—Adam Boulton, Political editor, Sky News

"A government cannot be scrutinised too much or it is liable to make poor decisions. This Government went to war on a whim and a prayer. In the Gilligan affair, it is clearly to blame and has hounded an innocent person. Journalists are going to make mistakes—I made mistakes—but they should not be scared of doing their job. If anything, the media should be more robust."

—Martin Bell, Former BBC correspondent and ex-independent MP

"Politicians and the media have a lot to answer for. But the sound of the press attacking the BBC for distortion and spin is an irony too far. Journalists attack every institution but their own.

"We are paying a high price for forgetting the distinction between scepticism and cynicism. The remedy is simple: governments should play it straight, and the media should play it fair."

—Tony Wright MP, Chair of the Commons Public
Accounts Committee

"The culture of cynicism may soon turn into a culture of contempt. Ironically, the build-up to war showed a way forward— prime ministerial news conferences, select committee hearings and a genuine Commons vote all helped re-engage the public. My motto is: don't insult voters' intelligence if you don't want them to doubt your honesty."

—Nick Robinson, Political editor, ITV News

"The way we cover politics serves nobody well. Turnout at elections goes down. Do ordinary people enjoy the soundbites and the snarling? No. Look at how daily newspaper sales flattened in June through all the euro posturing.

"But Britain's robust media culture is something to be proud of, too. Compare the lack of scrutiny of policies post 9/11 in the US and the far lower level of newspaper readership in most of Europe.

"So where do we go from here? Calm down. Stop shouting. Remember that everyone is a human being. Remember that press proprietors are just as much self-interested in spin as anyone in Number 10. And realise the harm we're doing to ourselves. This situation isn't structural, merely increasingly demented."

—Peter Preston, Observer media commentator and
former *Guardian* editor

"Alastair Campbell's parting gift to Tony Blair may be that his leaving allows the Prime Minister to announce the dawn of a more honest, unspun era. But making Campbell the bogeyman misses the point: both journalists and government are responsible for our dysfunctional relationship.

"How to repair it? Politicians could be more honest: confess when they get it wrong, stop promising the impossible, resist the temptation to be too clever. But this will only work if journalists stop pouncing on anyone who dares admit weakness, and start chasing stories—such as why we went to war—rather than scalps like Campbell's."

—Gaby Hinsliff, Chief political correspondent,
the *Observer*

"The corrosive, parochial media-politicians relationship is disconnected from the people. I blame the political classes, who have become obsessed with spin. We do have a robust media, and so we should. Politicians should get away from Westminster and focus on the many important political meetings and campaigns up and down the country."

—Mark Seddon, Editor, *Tribune*

"This is a real crisis. The culture of the media, particularly of newspapers, corrodes public understanding of, and engagement in, politics. There are key problems: over-concentrated media ownership, a refusal to separate factual material from comment, and the assumption that all politicians are venal. Two have at least partial remedies: media ownership laws which forbid current levels of concentration; and a legal requirement to label, and therefore separate, news and comment. The third would require a compact between politicians and journalists. I fear this is beyond both sides."

—Michael Jacobs, General secretary, the Fabian Society

"A free press is important to ensure free speech. It is a love-hate relationship between us, but politicians and the media need to be honest and not indulge in spin to interest people in politics."

—Theresa May, Chair, the Conservative Party

"It is worth bearing in mind that but for our robust media the public simply wouldn't know about the deception, carelessness and straight mendacity involved in the Government's preparation of the two Iraq dossiers. Campbell's assertion that 'something has gone wrong with our political and media culture' is special pleading. What he really means is 'please stop reporting government lies and incompetence.'"

—Peter Oborne, Political editor, the *Spectator*

"Voters are turned off by the Westminster game so loved by politicians and the media. They want politicians to be less adversarial, to speak to them in their own language, to listen more and to stop promising what they can't deliver."

—Sam Younger, Chair, Electoral Commission

"Politics needs to be less secretive. There is nothing wrong with people like Dr Kelly speaking to journalists. But I hate seeing so many sources not being attributed: it looks very suspicious. Campbell decides what to leak and to whom: journalists have to ask, why is this source giving me the story?"

—Sheila Gunn, Former press secretary to John Major

"Spin degrades journalism as well as politics. Spin works because journalists queue up for briefings from those who are seen to be close to power. They are kept in line with leaks, prior announcements and background briefings. Those who refuse to toe the line are deprived of access. Spin meisters enhance their power by demonstrating their 'control' of the media. Their advice is taken before policy is decided. Through background briefing they puff or weaken politicians and thus extend their influence.

"Before long the announcements are the policy and the media-friendly politicians the leaders, and the quality of decision making deteriorates. Marshall McLuhan foresaw this. The medium is now the message and everything is degraded. The solution is engraved on his tombstone: 'The truth will set you free.'"

—Clare Short MP, Former Secretary of State for
International Development

"The media and politics are two tectonic plates. Their stable co-existence is essential for a modern democracy. My worry is that self-regulation, either by the PCC or the BBC governors, is losing support but the alternative of statutory regulation by OFCOM would be the end of the free press as we know it. Perhaps there is a case for some sort of independent commission to produce a new Concordat that can survive these big events."

—Charles Lewington, Managing Director, Media Strategy and former Director, Conservative Central Office

"I think in the end the emphasis on spin misses the point. This is the product of an unreconstructed and unreformed society. All the same problems that were thrown up by John Major's government—in terms of the public finding out what's going on—are thrown up again. There has to be a root and branch solution: we need a wholesale and complete freedom of information act."

—Jon Snow, Channel Four news

"The relationship between politics and the media should never be cosy. It does not matter if the relationship is one of conflict—they have different jobs. There is a danger that both politicians and journalists become overly influenced by media owners who have a purely commercial interest and are only interested in pursuing a profit agenda, rather than any democratic or journalistic effort. As long as the journalist is working in the pursuit of truth and accountability then it does not matter how robust they are and they have to be weary of owners who can prostitute the profession."

—Lord McNally, LibDem peer

"*The institute will seek to become a recognised and impartial authority on all aspects of journalism; to attain the highest standards in academic research, but also to respond quickly to current debates; and to chart the technological, economic and market changes which influence news media today.*"

The Media Needs a Watchdog

Geert Linnebank

In the following viewpoint Geert Linnebank argues that only through media watchdogs and self-scrutiny with an open mind for change can the media remain truly independent from government and other interference. Written nearly a decade ago, the viewpoint reflects the approval of the author that his news organization, Reuters, had moved toward self-reflection and betterment. The author also expresses the hope that more in the media would follow suit. Geert Linnebank was editor-in-chief of Reuters from 2006 to 2006 and is a member of the Reuters Institute Steering Committee and Editorial Committee.

"Journalism Ethics: An Unbiased, Watchful Eye," by Geert Linnebank, The Independent, Helen Mars @ Independent, January 23, 2006. Reprinted by permission.

As you read, consider the following questions:

1. How have times changed in regard to media self-reflection since this article was written in 2006?
2. Is the author's optimism about Reuters well founded based on the hopes he expresses here?
3. What threats to free speech can be expected if media watchdogs are put in place to try to guarantee media fairness?

Even in an era of mass access to the internet and the meteoric rise of "citizen journalism," the power of the traditional media to shape opinion is a fact of modern life. It is acknowledged, discussed, criticised and sometimes lamented, but very rarely forensically examined. Journalists, once content to be informed bystanders, increasingly now take their place in the ranks of leading public figures, setting news agendas and political tone while arbitrating on issues of trust and truth using the media's own yardsticks.

At Reuters we have never embraced celebrity journalism. Perhaps because of that, and because of our role as a primary and unbiased source of global news, we are not afraid to ask the question raised in the Latin phrase "quis custodiet ipsos custodes"—who will guard the guardians?

I believe it is natural at Reuters for us to ask this question. We ourselves are governed in our daily news coverage by Reuters Trust Principles, our equivalent to a constitution, which guarantees independence from pressures by government, shareholders, institutions or other interest groups. We know that one of the best ways to ensure independence is to scrutinise ourselves and to accept the scrutiny of others. The recently announced plans to create the Reuters Institute for the Study of Journalism at Oxford University flow naturally from this belief. In an initiative funded with £1.75m over five years by the Reuters Foundation, our charitable arm, the aim is to establish a research centre of excellence in the study of journalism in all its forms. The Institute will be an integral part

POLITICS AND MEDIA: THE EVOLUTION OF A RELATIONSHIP

During the recent Republication debates in Colorado, I found myself thinking about the relationship between the dominant media of the time and politicians. There is a symbiotic relationship here we cannot ignore—they really need each other to succeed. The relationship between politics and the media has evolved over time, but has it changed for the better?

The emergence of cable television programming in the 1980s redefined the relationship between politicians and the media once again. C-SPAN gave us an unprecedented look into our political system and new networks defined their existence around partisan politics. More than ever before, news came with a party affiliation and the tag of liberal or conservative. CNN, true to its original mission, sits in the middle with a strong following, but the existence of spin rooms and dissecting the candidates into "what he/she meant to say" became stronger than ever.

In recent years, we have seen the emergence of high-speed broadband technologies that have changed our views once again. President Obama mastered social media with his last election and we understood the importance of this new medium. Television audiences see comments from social media on the screen in real time. Donald Trump finds that he gets so much exposure in the media he has not had to spend funds he set aside for advertising. We can watch the debates on our phone or iPad or watch them later on DVR. Polling is instantaneous from traditional and social media sources while the "talking heads" tell us what we were supposed to hear in case we missed it. Oh, brave new world …

At the end of the day, it always boils down to ratings for the media. For the candidates, it is a matter of getting their message out to the greatest number of people as efficiently as possible. The relationship between the politicians and media is as complicated as ever. It is also true that we get to evaluate the candidates better than ever before because of the innovative nature of our technology. This has been true in the past and is likely to continue well into the future.

"The Evolution of Politics and Media," Access Intelligence, LLC, October 29, 2015.

of Oxford University's Department of Politics and International Relations and will be based at Green College, bringing journalism formally within the university's field of academic study for the first time.

For Reuters, putting our name to an institute is much more than a marketing exercise. We live out our values of impartiality and accuracy in the thousands of news stories, photos and video clips we produce every day, but we also aim to improve the standards of good journalism globally. As just one example, recently Reuters Foundation was instrumental in establishing Iraq's first independent news agency, Aswat Al-Iraq, instilling a new generation of journalists with the fundamental tenets of honest, responsible and insightful reporting.

"Oh no—not more Professors of Journalism," I can hear some people saying. It is true to say there is no shortage of university media courses, at least in the UK. However, while the power of media has increased, the parallel rise in "media studies" has not fulfilled the requirement for analysis, debate and insight. Media departments in universities are mostly concerned with training in the norms of journalism and public relations, or with high theory or long-term research. While they certainly serve a purpose and the work often is of excellent quality, their output is usually regarded with disdain by the industry.

The Reuters Institute at Oxford is not an attempt to jump on the media studies bandwagon. It will not offer undergraduate degree courses but instead focus on supporting high-quality research, analysis and comment about how the media operates, and provide an independent forum for exchanges between practitioners and analysts of journalism and—no less important—all those affected by it. Only by focusing on engaging practitioners from every area of the news media and associated professions will we break down the incomprehension and distrust which have defined the relationship between academia and journalism.

To help this process, plans for the institute have been drawn up by figures drawn from both worlds. Tim Gardam, formerly of Channel 4 and the BBC, now Principal of St Anne's College, Oxford, has chaired the steering committee, which includes John Lloyd, contributing editor of the *Financial Times*. Bringing the academic and media worlds together is only part of the solution to improving the relationship. Another challenge lies in establishing the usefulness of research. News executives pay little heed to theoretical research, often viewing it as ivory tower navel-gazing with little relevance to the practicalities of a newsroom. For the Reuters Institute to succeed, its work must be rooted in the actual practice of journalism, rather than in the study of mass communications or political science.

The emphasis will be on engaging practitioners through publications, seminars, lectures and debates. But academics throwing open their doors is not enough; practitioners need to comprehend the value of research. The decline of public engagement in the US has been directly attributed to the decline in the attention to news, be it in print or broadcast, and while media organisations are both a culprit and victim of this decline, they are struggling with the consequences while ignoring the reasons.

The issue, then, is not to glamorise research in the hope of capturing attention, but to engage the media industry through covering both short and long-term trends and translate them into practical insight useful to their everyday operations and future success. We will aim to encourage and direct dialogue rather than produce dust-gathering research with little practical relevance. The institute will seek to become a recognised and impartial authority on all aspects of journalism; to attain the highest standards in academic research, but also to respond quickly to current debates; and to chart the technological, economic and market changes which influence news media today.

Reuters links to journalism insight or the academic world are not new. Since its creation in 1982, Reuters Foundation has trained more than 4,000 journalists from 170 countries in practical topics ranging from reporting business news to covering HIV/ Aids. In addition, the Reuters Foundation Journalism Fellowship

Programme, established at Oxford University for more than 20 years, has developed a reputation for attracting first-class journalists from across the world to engage in serious research. It has been one of the longest-standing international journalism institutions outside the US.

In truth the new institute will not be, or even aspire to be, a "guardian." But I believe that the unbiased, analytical light the institute will shed on the media's activities, good and bad, will prove to be an invaluable guide to all of us caught up in the daily rough and tumble of life in the modern media.

Periodical and Internet Sources Bibliography

The following articles have been selected to supplement the diverse views presented in this chapter.

Monika Bauerlein, "Journalism Is Imploding Just When We Need It Most," Mother Jones and the Foundation for National Progress, November 24, 2017. https://www.motherjones.com/politics/2017/11/journalism-is-imploding-just-when-we-need-it-most/.

Scott Conroy, "How young reporters can help revitalize political journalism in the Trump era," Huffington Post, January 18, 2017. https://www.huffingtonpost.com/entry/how-young-reporters-can-help-revitalize-political-journalism_us_587f8483e4b0c147f0bc0b9f.

John Friedman, "False 'news' should be treated as a defective and dangerous product," Huffington Post. Feabruary 27, 2015. https://www.huffingtonpost.com/john-friedman/false-news-should-be-trea_b_6768530.html.

Rick Gell, "Google and Facebook are major outlets for media—so why aren't they held accountable for spreading fake news?" Alternet, January 6, 2018. https://www.alternet.org/media/platform-vs-publisher-google-facebook-unaccountable-fake-news.

Jeff Guo, "The imminent takeover of local TV news, explained," Vox, May 15, 2017. https://www.vox.com/2017/5/15/15598270/sinclair-broadcast-imminent-conservative-takeover-of-local-tv-news-explained.

"Upset about political bias in the media? Blame economics," Wharton, May 22, 2013. http://knowledge.wharton.upenn.edu/article/upset-about-political-bias-in-the-media-blame-economics/.

Tamar Wilner, "We Can Probably Measure Media Bias. But Do We Want To?" Columbia Journalism Review, January 9, 2018. https://www.cjr.org/innovations/measure-media-bias-partisan.php.

OPPOSING
VIEWPOINTS®
SERIES

CHAPTER 3

Is There a Place for Morals in Politics Today?

Chapter Preface

The increased political polarization of the United States in recent years has taken on what many believe to be disturbing forms. It has motivated both politicians and the media to place partisan politics above truth and morality. What a political figure has done or expressed in the past is often glossed over or even ignored in an attempt to curry favor with voters or the party of choice.

The tactic often does not work with US voters, who still hold morality in high esteem. One example was President Trump's backing of Alabama senatorial candidate Roy Moore despite accusations against the candidate for past sexual improprieties against teenagers. Trump's support, seen as ironic given the charges made against him by women in the recent past, did not help Moore enough. In the reddest of red states, Moore lost to a middle-of-the-road Democrat.

Other prominent politicians and noted media members, some of which had based their careers on conservative morality, were cast aside as well in a spate of controversial allegations that were proven true. But many believe that the private lives of politicians should either remain private or not be used against them because they might not negatively influence their work. Bill Clinton is widely accepted as one of the most popular presidents of the modern era despite his affair with White House intern Monica Lewinsky and his initial denials of it. Some feel that the notion that all people, including politicians and news media stars, are only human and should not be judged any other way.

Others, however, believe that morality and job performance are inextricably linked. How public figures act in their private lives is an indicator of their worldview and potential relationships with constituents, viewers, or readers. The authors of the viewpoints in this chapter take varying stances on this issue.

| "*The GOP 'ought to be a party focused on principles.'*"

Backing an Alleged Criminal in Favor of His Political Party Is No Longer Inexcusable

Martin Pengelly

In the following viewpoint Martin Pengelly reports on the White House's backing of Alabama senate candidate Roy Moore. The substantial and disturbing allegations of Moore's sexual misconduct against young women over the years was all but ignored or glossed over by many Republicans in an attempt to keep a Democrat out of office. The most significant defender—or offender—was President Trump, who urged voters to back Moore despite the horrific charges. Their efforts proved to be in vain as Moore suffered a rare Republican defeat in that red state. Martin Pengelly is weekend editor for Guardian US.

As you read, consider the following questions:

1. What did the Republican backing of Roy Moore indicate about the state of American politics?
2. How many women accused Trump of sexual misconduct?
3. Which Republican leaders took the high moral road?

"Roy Moore: Politicians of Both Parties Call Trump's Response Too Weak," by Martin Pengelly, Guardian News and Media Limited, November 12, 2017. Reprinted by permission.

Politicians from both sides of the aisle said on Sunday Donald Trump's handling of allegations of sexual misconduct against Roy Moore, the Republican Senate candidate in Alabama, was not good enough and he should call for Moore to withdraw.

Appearing on CNN's State of the Union on Sunday, the US treasury secretary, Steven Mnuchin, repeated the White House line that was first articulated by the White House press secretary, Sarah Sanders.

"If the allegations prove to be true, he should step down," he said.

Dick Durbin, a Democratic senator from Illinois, countered that it was Trump's "responsibility to do more when it comes to this situation in Alabama."

John Kasich, the Republican governor of Ohio, agreed the White House response was not good enough and added that he had thought Moore, a hardline Christian conservative twice removed from his state's supreme court, "too divisive of a person to go … to the Senate" even before the allegations were made.

The *Washington Post* reported this week that an Alabama woman said Moore had sexual contact with her when she was 14 and he was a 32-year-old assistant district attorney. Three other women told the Post Moore had sexual contact with them when they were teenagers.

Moore, 70, has denied the allegations and said they were politically motivated. On Saturday, he told a Republican audience in a suburb of Birmingham: "In the next few days, there will be revelations about the motivations and the content of this article that will be brought to the public. We fully expect the people of Alabama to see through this charade."

On Air Force One on Saturday Trump, who is travelling in Asia, referred reporters to Sanders' original statement, although he did add that he did not know about Moore's case because he did "not watch much television."

Trump himself has been accused by least 16 women of sexual misconduct or assault. He has denied the allegations and Sanders said last month all those women were lying.

On Sunday, Mnuchin was asked if the weight of claims against Moore might be enough to disqualify him. He said: "I'm not an expert on this issue but what I would say is that people should investigate this issue and get the facts. And if these allegations are true, absolutely this is incredibly inappropriate behaviour."

Asked if he believed the four women, Mnuchin conceded that it "appears that there is a significant issue here that needs to be addressed."

Durbin and Kasich also spoke to CNN. Durbin said: "A lot of my Republican colleagues ... feel very passionately about this. They've spoken out on it and I respect them for doing it. It's time for the president to do the same."

Kasich, who fought Trump for the Republican presidential nomination, said: "Look, I wasn't for [Moore] in the beginning ... there's a growing list of people that think he ought to step aside and not be the standard bearer."

Moore, who has said "homosexual conduct should be illegal" and contended that the 9/11 attacks were a case of divine retribution, is backed by the populist wing of the Republican party, a force fuelled by the former Trump counsellor Steve Bannon.

In a week that saw Democratic gains in state and local elections, establishment figures including the Senate majority leader, Mitch McConnell, have called on Moore to step aside. Trump backed McConnell's preferred candidate in the primary, then switched his support to Moore.

Kasich continued: "So many people now in Alabama are saying: 'Yeah, we believe her,' and you have Republicans like John McCain, Mitt Romney, John Kasich saying he should step aside, [so] yes, of course he should [step down]."

Moore cannot be removed from the ballot in the 12 December special election, which will fill the seat vacated by the US attorney general, Jeff Sessions. Kasich would not say Alabamans should vote for Moore's Democratic opponent, Doug Jones, but he pointed to another Republican Senate election success against a populist insurgent.

He said: "I think he should step aside. If not maybe [we] can get a write-in candidate. Lisa Murkowski did it in Alaska, she was elected, I think she's urging somebody down there to do that."

Local Republicans have been supportive of Moore, who is strongly backed by evangelical voters. On Saturday, Albert Mohler, president of the Southern Baptist Theological Seminary in Louisville, Kentucky, told the Associated Press the allegations "if true, are devastating."

But he hinted at likely resilience among Moore supporters when he said that for evangelical voters "there's so much at stake. Those of us who are pro-life have got to be very concerned about losing even one seat in the US Senate."

Other Republicans also weighed in. Tim Scott, a senator from South Carolina, told CBS's *Face the Nation* Moore's "denial was not as strong as the allegations" and said the GOP "ought to be a party focused on principles."

Pat Toomey, a senator from Pennsylvania, told NBC's *Meet the Press* "the preponderance of the evidence seems to support the accuser" and said he "would prefer for Roy to step aside" in favour of a write-in candidate.

Like Kasich, Toomey would not be drawn on whether Republicans in the Senate should work with Moore if he is elected regardless.

"No democracy should make the price of public service the sacrifice of all one's rights, especially when the consequences may be permanent and follow the individual long after leaving office."

Politicians Have a Reasonable Right to Privacy

Dennis F. Thompson

In the following viewpoint Dennis F. Thompson compares French and American politics to argue that public disclosures of the personal vagaries of politicians could prove damaging to society. Thompson contends that such discourse removes the spotlight from far more important issues and that otherwise capable people with strong ideas might be removed from consideration simply because of weaknesses outside the realm of politics. Dennis F. Thompson is professor emeritus of political philosophy at Harvard University.

As you read, consider the following questions:

1. Does the author claim that personal issues of politicians should be ignored or discounted?
2. How does the author compare French and American politics?
3. What would be the counterargument in claiming that the personal lives of politicians should be taken seriously by voters and the media?

"The Private Life of Politicians," by Dennis F. Thompson, Raison-Publique.fr, February 6, 2010. Raison-Publique (2010)—Pre-Publication version. Reprinted by permission.

Politicians who wish to keep their private life private, it used to be confidently said, are safer in France than in the United States. The public attention to President Bill Clinton's sexual escapades is only the most dramatic of several decades of exposure the private lives of presidents, senators, candidates and state and local politicians. Sexual relationships, drinking habits, family troubles, personal health have been fair game for the American press at least since the exposure of presidential candidate Gary Hart's adultery in 1987. In contrast, the private lives of French politicians have long been assumed to be off limits. The affairs of Jacques Chirac and François Mitterrand were not widely reported, and attracted little coverage when finally publicized (even though Mitterrand was supporting a second family, partly at government expense).

For many years, France and the US represented polar paradigms of the privacy of politicians. Other European countries stood between the poles though most lay closer to France than to the US. This sharp contrast is now fading, as France and other countries begin to succumb to many of the same forces that have shaped public discourse in the United States.[1] Candidates increasingly open their personal lives to the press. Nicholas Sarkozy talked openly about his marital difficulties. Ségolène Royal's childbirth, her "free" marriage, and even her techniques for dealing with cellulite became prominent stories. The erosion of the boundaries between the private and the public in politics is eroding in most democracies.

No doubt the trend has many causes—the increasing competition in the media, the personalization of political campaigns, the expansion of the internet, among other forces that are shaping democratic politics in the globalized society. And no doubt the trend will continue despite the persistent criticism of some commentators and the occasional disapproval of some citizens. But this escalating publicization of private life should be resisted as far as possible. It gains more legitimacy than it deserves from mistaken assumptions about the basis of privacy of politicians, and about the nature of criteria that could justify publicizing their private lives. The reason to resist this trend, I wish to argue, is to protect not the rights of privacy of politicians but the integrity of the democratic process.

The Rights of Politicians

Privacy involves the protection of information about an individual that he or she is entitled to control: personal activities that should not be known, observed, or intruded upon without his or her consent. The most common justification for this claim invokes the right of privacy that all citizens should possess. Like all politicians, officials have some right to the kind of control implied by this right. No democracy should make the price of public service the sacrifice of all one's rights, especially when the consequences may be permanent and follow the individual long after leaving office.

Although political culture in the United States is generally thought to be more rights-centered than in other democracies, its norms and laws protect the privacy rights of politicians less. The contrast with France is especially striking. In addition to cultural and professional norms against publicizing private lives, French law threatens severe sanctions for violations of privacy rights (violations of the intimité de la view privée even more severely than the vie privée).[2] Unlike US jurisprudence, French law does not sharply distinguish between the rights of public figures such as politicians or celebrities, and those of ordinary citizens. Even photographs of public figures are subject to protection by means of the droit à l'image: the images are treated as private property.

Another (related) justification for privacy of politicians refers to effects on the recruitment. If the press constantly probes the private lives of politicians, some worthy candidates may be discouraged from running for office. The prospect of exposing to public scrutiny one's personal finances (and those of one's family) or any past indiscretion (however minor) is hardly a positive incentive to seek public office. This justification at least has the virtue of pointing to an effect on the democratic process—the potential loss of talented officials. But it still rests on an individual right. Until we decide how extensive a right of privacy a politician should have, we cannot assess whether an individual is warranted in avoiding public service. If someone declines to serve because he is claiming more than he has a right to, then he is not likely to be the kind of person we should want to hold public office.

Although many complain about the glare of publicity, many more continue to seek public office in spite of it. The question is not whether some decide not to seek office because of the possibility of public exposure, but which kinds of people decide not to seek office because of it. No doubt some admirable citizens who would be fine public servants decline to serve. But certainly some less admirable citizens, who have much to hide, decline to serve because they fear that their past (and present) transgressions may come to light. If the latter group is larger (and the number of quality people who are willing to serve does not diminish), we should consider the prospect of public exposure a favorable effect on recruitment.

However, grounding privacy on individual rights, especially without distinguishing between public officials and ordinary citizens, is misconceived. Citizens become public officials by choice: they may be presumed to consent to whatever limitations on their privacy are reasonably believed to be necessary for the effective functioning of the democratic process. What their rights are should depend on what these limitations are. What the democratic process requires should determine what rights officials have. Moreover, giving politicians such a strong right of privacy also gives them greater control over the public discourse than is desirable for healthy democratic debate. The "familialization of political life" and the "publicization of the private," according to some commentators, has already contributed to the "dumbing down" of political debate in France.[3] (In the personal diary kept during the 2002 campaign, Sylviane Agacinski (candidate Lionel Jospin wife) complained that the media's obsessive interest in candidates' spouses and partners led to the "trivialization of political debate."[4] Some commentators complained that her own actions contributed to the trivialization.

The Demands of Democratic Accountability

The common failing of any justifications based on the rights of politicians is that it does not connect the rationale for privacy to the needs of the democratic process.[5] Once we recognize that public officials do not have the same rights as ordinary citizens, the right to privacy argument does not provide much help in determining what the limits on publicity of politicians' lives should be.

Any adequate justification for privacy must rely on a view about what the democratic process requires. Although there are many different conceptions of democracy, we can posit a minimal requirement that should be acceptable on almost any conception. The requirement is *accountability*: citizens should be able to hold public officials accountable for their decisions and policies, and therefore citizens must have information that would enable them to judge how well officials are doing or are likely to do their job.[6]

It should sufficiently clear that the requirement of accountability provides a reason to override or diminish the right of privacy that officials would otherwise have. The requirement would clearly justify making some conduct public that is ordinarily private, such as information about mental or physical health that could affect performance, the finances of family members that could create conflicts of interest, and other activities that directly affect performance in public office.

But the accountability requirement has another implication that is less noticed but no less important. The requirement provides a reason to *limit* publicity about private lives. When such publicity undermines the practice of accountability, it is not justified. How can publicity undermine accountability? The most important way is through the operation of a political version of Gresham's law: Cheap talk drives out quality talk. (The mechanism itself is not quite analogous. The cheap talk dominates not because people hoard the quality talk in the hope that they might be able to enjoy it later, as Gresham thought people would hoard higher-value currency. Rather, the cheap talk attracts readers and viewers, even those who in their more reflective hours would prefer quality talk.)

Talk about private lives is "cheap" in two ways. First, the information is usually more immediately engaging and more readily comprehensible than information about job performance. Most people (understandably) think they know more about sex than tariffs. Second, the information itself is less reliable because it is usually less accessible and less comprehensive. Even if citizens happen to know more about the private lives of politicians than their public decisions, they may not be able to make reliable judgments about the effects of private conduct on public decisions. To make those kinds of judgments in a present case, they need information about past cases to establish reliable generalizations about the effects of private conduct on public performance. That kind of information is usually not readily available.

Given these characteristics, information about private life tends to dominate other forms of information and to lower the overall quality of public discourse and democratic accountability. Informing citizens about some matters makes it harder for them to be informed about other matters. To take a salient example: Even during the first six months of its public life, the Clinton-Lewinsky affair dominated media discussion of not only important new policy proposals on social security, health insurance, and campaign finance reform but also attempts to explain the US position on Iraq in preparation for military action.[7]

Journalists argue that they are only responding to what the public wants, and if the only test is what the public reads or views they may be right. But the considered judgments of most citizens in this and similar cases is that they do not need to know so much about the sexual affairs of their leaders[8] and that the press pays too much attention to their private lives.[9] It is perfectly consistent to believe that the political process would be better with less publicity about such matters, and even to prefer to know less about them, while at the same time eagerly reading whatever the press reports about them.

The Relevance of Private Life to Public Office

Democratic accountability permits some exposure of the private lives of officials if such information is necessary for assessing past or likely future performance in office. This is the basis of a familiar "relevance" standard: private conduct should be publicized to the extent that it is relevant to the performance in public office. But an essential point, often neglected in applying this standard, is that relevance is a matter of degree. The standard does not draw a bright line between private and public life, which would allow that once the conduct is deemed relevant it may be legitimately publicized without limit. The standard, properly interpreted, seeks a proportionate balance between degree of relevance and extent of publicity. We can see more clearly how this should be understood by considering the criteria that should guide decisions about what facts to publicize about the private lives of public officials even when the facts are presumptively relevant. These criteria (necessary conditions) may also be regarded as a series of questions that must be answered satisfactorily before otherwise private conduct of politicians may be legitimately made public.

How public is the conduct?

This criterion involves two different ways in which conduct can be public—the extent to which it is already known, and the extent to which it may be presented as requiring a governmental response. Simply because a matter is known to some journalists and some citizens is not a sufficient justification for publicizing it more widely. That Mitterand had an illegitimate daughter was common knowledge in Paris newsrooms for many decades but was not publicized until a year before he left office. One editor said later of the silence: "In retrospect, it was a mistake, because Mitterand was devoting significant government resources to his daughter."[10] Notice that the editor's justification does not appeal to the fact that the Mitterand's conduct was well known but that it was relevant to his job.

Similarly, the fact that the story is likely to be published elsewhere ("If we don't run it, somebody else will") is not in itself sufficient. With this justification, almost any story can be considered legitimate, whether actually public already or imminently so. The respectable press often tries to avoid the dilemma violating privacy and missing a story by a technique that may be called *metareporting*: writing about the fact that the less respectable press is writing about private scandals. Thus the *New York Times* (Scott 1998) publishes a story about unsubstantiated rumors that the *Daily News* has published about Clinton and Lewinsky—complete with miniature reproductions of the front pages of the News. This technique might be less problematic if the respectable press were not inclined to engage in metareporting about stories that feature sex so much more than about stories that reveal other failings of their fellow journalists.

To be sure, some sexual conduct should be publicized more than it is. Sexual harassment is not a private matter. Sexual conduct that would otherwise be private becomes a legitimate subject for investigation and reporting by the press when it violates the law, or violates what should be the law. Although the greater tolerance and sophistication that the French compared to Americans show toward sexual behavior is widely admired, it has a darker side. The French press publicizes cases of sexual harassment much less frequently than the US press, and more often treats those it does publicize as stories of abuses in personal relationships rather than as examples of discrimination that affect professional careers.[11] The French publicity also tends to be less sympathetic to the woman in the case, more often than in the US press framing the story as one about "greedy plaintiffs trying to get rich in lawsuits." According to a recent analysis, sexual seduction practiced by male politicians, "far from being a flaw ... is almost a civic imperative ... to cast yourself in the role of seducer is without a doubt an important quality in our political life."[12]

How public the conduct is, it should now be clear, depends not only on how widely it is known. It also depends substantially on how it is presented when it is publicized.

How extensive is the character defect?

A second criterion is that the private conduct must reveal a substantial character defect that is relevant to the job. Citizens may reasonably want to know, for example, about someone's tendency toward domestic violence when he is responsible for enforcing the law and regulating the finances of other people. But the appeal to character must be more specific than the common use of the character argument, which is undiscriminatingly general. The general claim that private conduct reveals character flaws that are bound eventually to show up on the job is a psychological version of the classical idea of the unity of the virtues. It assume that a person who mistreats his wife is likely to mistreat his colleagues; or that a person who does not control his violent temper is not likely to resist the temptation to lie.

We should be wary of this argument because many people, especially politicians, are quite capable of compartmentalizing their lives in the way that the idea of the unity of virtues denies. Indeed, for some people, private misbehavior may be cathartic, enabling them to behave better in public. And private virtue is no sign of public virtue. We should remember that most of the leading Watergate conspirators in the Nixon administration led impeccable private lives. So did most of the nearly 100 political appointees who were indicted or charged with ethics offenses during the early years of the Reagan administration.[13]

As far as character is concerned, we should be primarily interested in the political virtues—respect for the law and Constitution, a sense of fairness, honesty in official dealings. These virtues may not be correlated at all with personal ones. And the vices in which the press seems most interested—the sins of sex—are those that are probably least closely connected with the political vices.

Character is sometimes thought to be relevant in a different, more symbolic way. Officials represent us by who they are as much as by what they do. We need to know if they have the character fit for moral leadership—for serving as role models for our youth and virtuous spokespersons for our nation. But this conception of public office is too demanding, as most citizens seem to recognize. They seek leaders whose characters display the political virtues (such as honesty), but most do not believe that even the president should be held to higher moral standards in his private life than are ordinary citizens. [14] The question is not whether it would be desirable to have a leader who is as moral in his private as in his public life, but whether it is worth the sacrifice of privacy and the distortions of public debate that would be required to make private probity a job qualification.

How legitimate is the public reaction?
Private conduct may affect job performance not only because of what the officials themselves do but also because of the reactions of other people when they find out about the conduct. In the early days of the Clinton-Lewinsky scandal, many people said that although they themselves did not think the conduct was relevant to his performance, the expectation that other people, including foreign leaders, would have less confidence in him made it relevant.

But we need to be careful about appealing to reactive effects. The anticipated reaction of other people should almost never count as a sufficient reason to publicize further what would otherwise be private. The missing step in the argument—the factor that is often ignored—is the assumption that the private conduct itself is morally wrong, and that therefore the anticipated reactions of other people are morally justified.

Why this step is essential can be seen more clearly if we consider cases of homosexuals in public office being outed. The fact that constituents will vote against their conservative congressman if they find out he is gay is surely not a reason for publicizing his sexual orientation. Exploiting popular prejudices for political gain is not a practice that a worthy democracy should favor. However, the press probably should have written earlier than they did about the conduct of Representative Mark Foley, who was forced to resign in September, 2006. For many years he had sent on solicitant e-mails and sexually explicit instant messages to the teenage pages who work in Congress, and allegedly had sexual encounters with former pages. Foley was chairman of the House Caucus on Missing and Exploited Children, which introduced legislation targeting sexual predators and created stricter guidelines for tracking them. But the justification for the exposure of this and other such cases should not be that these politicians deserved to be punished for their hypocrisy or even that hypocrisy is in itself inexcusable, but that their hypocrisy is serving a morally wrong cause.[15]

If we invoke reactive effects when applying the relevance standard, we cannot escape making substantive moral judgments. Even when editors decide to disclose on the grounds that citizens themselves should decide whether the conduct is justifiable, they are in effect judging that the anticipated reactions are not bad enough to outweigh the value of informing citizens about the conduct. Once the story is out, the decision has been made. Without judging to what extent the reactions they are anticipating are justifiable, editors (and citizens more generally) will not be able to distinguish between outing a homosexual and exposing a wife beater.

How distracting is the disclosure?

The last criterion relates private conduct to other public issues. To what extent does knowing about this conduct help or hinder citizens' knowing about *other* matters they need to know to hold officials accountable? The focus is on the Gresham effects: is cheap talk driving out quality talk? Even when private vices bear some relation to the duties of public office, public discussions of politicians' ethics have an unfortunate tendency to dwell on private conduct to the neglect of conduct more relevant to the office. In the confirmation hearings of Clarence Thomas, the press, the public, and the Senate Judiciary Committee paid more attention to Clarence Thomas's relationship with Anita Hill than to his judicial qualifications. The Gresham effects are especially damaging when, as in this case, irreversible decisions are made under tight constraints of time, so that any distortions in the process of accountability cannot be corrected as they might be in the normal course of politics.

The Gresham effects go well beyond particular cases such as Clarence Thomas and Bill Clinton. The cumulative consequences of many cases, as they increase in number and prominence, create a pattern of press coverage that distorts our common practices of deliberation. Habits of discourse—the considerations we easily identify, the distinctions we readily make, the reasons we immediately accept—become better adapted to controversies about private life than to public life. The more citizens hone their skills of deliberation on the finer points of sexual encounters (would he have really put her hand there?), the less they are prepared to develop their capacities to deliberate about the nuances of public policy (should he support this revision of the welfare program?). Democratic deliberation is degraded, and democratic accountability thereby eroded.

Publicity about the private lives of public officials can damage the democratic process by distracting citizens from more important questions of policy and performance of government. When deciding whether to publicize what would otherwise be private conduct or when judging such decisions made by others, including the press and officials themselves, the key questions concern the effects on accountability. Is the conduct of a type about which citizens generally need to know in order to hold officials in this position accountable? If the conduct is relevant in this sense, is the degree of the publicity proportionate to the relevance? Are the character flaws revealed by the conduct closely and specifically connected to the office (are they political rather than only personal vices)? If negative public reaction to the conduct is part of the reason for publicizing it, is the reaction morally justified? Is the publicity about the conduct unlikely to distract citizens from paying attention to other political matters they need to know to hold officials accountable (will there be no Gresham effects)? If more citizens, journalists, and officials themselves would more often consider these questions seriously, and more regularly restrain their penchant for publicity when they cannot honestly answer them in the affirmative, we might notice some improvement in the quality of democratic discourse. In the meantime, citizens in the US and increasingly in Europe will remain hostage to the vagaries of a political version of Gresham's law.

Notes

* This article is based on "Private Life and Public Office," in Restoring Responsibility: Ethics in Government, Business and Healthcare, Cambridge University Press, 2004.

1. For a useful survey and comparison of trends in the U.S. and European democracies, see "Public Images, Private Lives: The Mediation of Politicians around the Globe," special issue of Parliamentary Affairs, 57 (January 2004).

2. Helen Trouille, "Private Life and Public Image: Privacy Legislation in France," International and Comparative Law Quarterly, 49, January 2000, p. 199-208; and Raymond Kuhn, "'Vive La Différence'? The Mediation of Politicians' Public Images and Private Lives in France," Parliamentary Affairs, 57 (January 2004), pp. 24-40.

3. Kuhn, pp. 34-35.

4. Ibid.

5. Although Thomas Nagel justifies politician's privacy in part by appealing to individual rights (privacy is necessary to protect against "gross invasion of the individual's personal life"), he emphasizes equally the importance of protecting the public space from "unmanageable encroachment and uncontrollable conflict and offense" (Concealment and Exposure, Oxford, Oxford University Press, 2002, pp. 28-29).

6. For analysis of the principle as part of deliberative democracy, see Amy Gutmann and Dennis Thompson, Democracy and Disagreement, Cambridge, Cambridge University Press, 1996, pp. 128-164. Also see the discussion of "publicity" at pp. 95-127.

7. A comparative content analysis of the press coverage of Gary Hart in the 1988 campaign and Bill Clinton in 1992 found that the stories of the affairs dominated the coverage of Hart's campaign though the coverage "did not fully eclipse" discussion of Clinton's stand on issues because the press "cast more doubt on the accuser, Gennifer Flowers, and the medium, The Star" (J. G. Payne and K. Mercuri, "Private Lives, Public Officials: The Challenge to Mainstream Media," American Behavioral Scientist, 37, November 1993, pp. 298).

8. Sixty-four percent of respondents in a February 1998 survey said it is not important for the public to know "what the relationship was" between Clinton and Lewinsky. Distinguishing the relationship from legal testimony about it, 61 percent said it is important for the public to know whether Clinton encouraged Lewinsky to lie (J. Bennet with J. Elder, "Despite Intern, President Stays in Good Graces," New York Times, February 24, 1998, pp. Al, A16).

9. In a 1998 Roper Center national survey, 80 percent of the respondents said they thought the media coverage of the Clinton-Lewinsky story was "excessive." Sixty percent agreed with the more general proposition that the media have "gone too far in disclosing the details of Clinton's private life," while only 9 percent thought the media had not gone "far enough" (Roper Center for Survey Research and Analysis, Clinton-Lewinsky News Coverage [conducted January 30–February 4], Public Opinion Online, Storrs, Conn.: University of Connecticut, February 6, 1998). Even before this scandal, 60 percent of respondents in 1994 said that the news media pay too much attention to Clinton's private life (Roper Center, Princeton Survey Research Associates, Newsweek, conducted May 6, Public Opinion Online, Storrs, Conn.: University of Connecticut, May 1994.) Since the 1980s there has been a steady and substantial increase in the number of people who say that the "increased attention being given to the private lives of public officials and candidates" is a "bad thing"— from 39 percent in 1989 to 47 percent in 1993 (Gallup Organization, Gallup, Newsweek, conducted June 1–2, 1989; March 9-10, 1993, Public Opinion Online, Storrs, Conn.: University of Connecticut, June 1989; and March 1993).

10. Britta Sandberg, "A Taboo is Broken: French Politics Go Populist," Spiegel Online, October 17, 2006.

11. Abigail C. Saguy, What is Sexual Harassment?: From Capitol Hill to the Sorbonne, Berkeley, University of California Press, 2003.

12. Christophe Dubois and Christophe Deloire, Sexus Politicus, Albin Michel, 2006, quoted by Elaine Sciolino, "Sex and the Path to Power in France," New York Times, October 16, 2006.

13. G. Lardner, Jr., "Conduct Unbecoming an Administration," Washington Post National Weekly Edition, (January 3, 1988), pp. 31-32.

14. About 53 percent of the respondents in a national survey in 1998 in the aftermath of the Lewinsky publicity said that "when it comes to conduct in one's personal life," the president should be held to the same standard you hold yourself, while 44 percent said he should be held to a higher standard. An overwhelming majority, 84 percent, agree that "someone can still be a good President even if they do things in their personal life that you disapprove of" (Roper Center, CBS News, New York Times, conducted February 19–21, Public Opinion Online, Storrs, Conn.: University of Connecticut, February 23, 1998).

15. If the politician flagrantly and for no public purpose disregards moral sensitivities, in effect inviting scrutiny of private conduct that offends many people, the press may be justified in exposing it, whether or not it is in itself seriously wrong. The politician is guilty of failing to take into account the reasonable reactions of citizens. Politicians who behave in such ways display a form of the traditional vice of "giving scandal" (Thomas Aquinas, Question 43, "Scandal." in T. C. O'Brien, ed. and trans., Virtues of Justice in the Human Community, London: Blackfriars, 1972, vol. 35, pp. 109-137).

| "By concealing the affairs of the past, journalists unwittingly created the impression that modern sex scandals are a new phenomenon."

Place the Blame on a Scandal-Mongering Press

Ross Benes

In the following viewpoint Ross Benes argues in favor of a free, independent and curious press. He cites the administrations of Roosevelt, Kennedy, Nixon, and Clinton to examine how the media has covered the private lives of US politicians to varying effect throughout history. The author contends that journalists should provide a window to the past to give context to what is happening on the present. Ross Benes is a Digiday *reporter who has written for the* Wall Street Journal, Rolling Stone, Refinery29, Deadspin, Quartz, Slate, Vice, *and* Esquire.

As you read, consider the following questions:

1. Does the author believe it was wrong for politicians of the past to get a pass for personal issues from the media?
2. How does the viewpoint look at American politics in a timeline and what conclusion are drawn from it?
3. What level of importance does the author indicate he has in regard to a free press investigating and reporting personal issues of politicians?

"Why Do America's Private Affairs Explode into Scandal? Blame the Press," by Ross Benes, The Poynter Institute, May 15, 2017. Reprinted by permission.

From the founding fathers through John F. Kennedy and Bill Clinton, American politicians have indulged in extramarital affairs with slaves, movie stars, sisters-in-law and interns.

But, in large part because of the press, the American public still reacts to political sex scandals as if they were completely unheard of.

Americans remain shocked by these events, I believe, in large part because our perception has been shaped more by the press's behavior than by the behavior of the politicians themselves. While putting together my book *The Sex Effect*, I found a connection between the way journalists cover extramarital affairs and the public's opinion on sexual matters.

Although the press has generally tried to expose public figures since Watergate, the media's approach to uncovering the dirty secrets of politicians has fluctuated throughout American history.

One of the first major political sex scandals in the US involved Alexander Hamilton and a married woman named Maria Reynolds. America's first secretary of the treasury was so enamored with Reynolds that he paid her husband, James Reynolds, to keep the relationship secret.

In the end, though, Hamilton's affair was exposed by a zealous pamphleteer named James Callender. Callender and his contemporaries were more like activist bloggers than nonpartisan journalists.

"Most pamphlets were written to appeal to some certain emotion or to some particular group of people," wrote historian Homer Calkin. "Patriotic, religious and economic motives often formed the theme of a pamphleteer."

The writing in these pamphlets was often extremely ideological because political parties and people with financial power used pamphlets as propaganda tools. After Callender broke the Hamilton-Reynolds scandal, he was hired by Thomas Jefferson to target Jefferson's political opponent John Adams. But Callender and Jefferson had a falling out, so Callender revealed that Jefferson had a sexual relationship with his teenage slave, Sally Hemings.

MUST PRESIDENTS BE ROLE MODELS?

Michelle Obama says Donald Trump is no role model—but do presidents need to be role models? Trump supporters argue that he's the hero America needs. He's imperfect, but he is a leader who will make the necessary changes to make America great again. Others think that the role of president goes far beyond governance. The oval office is a powerful symbol of what America wants and chooses to be.

Let's face it: presidents are politicians, and politicians rarely make good role models. That's just the nature of the job. While the office of the presidency is incredibly important, let's not idealize the past. There have been presidents who have done truly reprehensible things and have held vile opinions. What's more important is what a president achieves in their term. Their character is secondary.

This whole "role model" question reveals one of the limitations of democracy. Because our leaders can only rule by our consent, we ignore their obvious flaws—their egos, their vanities, their ignorance—because not doing so would make it impossible for us to vote for anyone.

Then, once we elect these fairly average human beings, we expect them to transcend our petty differences and solve the intractable problems that make our lives difficult. But that's not humanly possible. So we should stop even debating whether they are role models. They are not.

It would be preferable to have a president who was a good person. But maybe there's an upside to the election of a president who so many Americans see as deeply morally flawed. Every president and his defenders try to blur the line between the man and the office: sneer at the man and they'll accuse you of disrespecting the office—casually ignoring how the president disrespected the public.

When America votes for a president, it votes for an ideal, for the direction they want America to go. The office of the presidency is ceremonial, it is about upholding American ideals.

"Do Presidents Need to Be Role Models?" The Tylt.

Jefferson's sex scandal was opened to public scrutiny by the sensational media standards of the day. For example, an 1828 *Cincinnati Gazette* story about Andrew Jackson screamed, "General Jackson's mother was a COMMON PROSTITUTE, brought to this country by British soldiers! She afterward married a MULATTO MAN with whom she had several children, of which General JACKSON IS ONE!!!"

But media coverage of politicians' personal lives gradually shifted. During the Great Depression, World War I, World War II and the Cold War, US journalists opted to forego sensational stories about the personal lives of leaders, preferring instead to focus their reporting on matters of national security. By the time Franklin Roosevelt became president, journalists often kept politicians' secrets hidden in exchange for access. Historians also theorize that journalists protected politicians' personal lives during this time as a matter of national security.

With the uncertainty brought on by the Great Depression and World War II, journalists decided to help conceal Roosevelt's personal life. Millions of Americans didn't realize he was paralyzed until after his death. Today, few photos exist of Roosevelt in a wheelchair.

Journalists also concealed Roosevelt's sexual relationships. Many Americans still are unaware that Roosevelt had numerous affairs. According to Joseph Persico's *Franklin and Lucy: Mrs. Rutherford and the Other Remarkable Women in Roosevelt's Life,* which details Roosevelt's affairs, journalists who supported Roosevelt prevented other reporters from photographing the president in his wheelchair.

Journalists blocked or knocked aside photographers who tried to shoot images of the president's disability. In newspapers, cartoonists portrayed Roosevelt as a superhero. If ever cameras began rolling when he was lifted out of his wheelchair, Roosevelt said things like, "No movies of me getting out of the machine, boys." Journalists often respected the request.

Like Roosevelt, President Kennedy benefitted from a comfortable relationship with the press. Despite all that we now know about Kennedy's numerous affairs, he never had a public sex scandal while in office, in large part because of the press.

"Before Watergate, reporters just didn't go into that sort of thing," said a Hollywood Associated Press writer who helped keep Kennedy's affair with Marilyn Monroe out of the press. "I'd have to have been under the bed in order to put it on the wire for the AP."

Not long after Kennedy was assassinated, President Johnson ramped up America's involvement in the Vietnam War, an action that led to years of anti-government protests. Fewer than 10 years after Kennedy's death, the presidency faced the greatest scandal in its history with Watergate, which led to President Nixon's resignation. These events made journalists more aware of their duties to inform the public of unsavory deeds. Reporters undertook a renewed effort to expose secrets as they did in the pamphleteering era.

"Between the Kennedy and the Clinton presidencies, access journalism was replaced by gotcha journalism," wrote historian David Eisenbach and *Hustler* publisher Larry Flynt in their book, *One Nation Under Sex.*

By Bill Clinton's second term, 24/7 news networks and the growing power of the internet gave reporters tools to spread indiscretions faster. The world became more connected, and journalists were more aggressive. When Matt Drudge exposed Clinton's affair with Monica Lewinsky, he wasn't doing anything radical. By then, any journalist would have craved that tip.

By concealing the affairs of the past, journalists unwittingly created the impression that modern sex scandals are a new phenomenon. Not all sex scandals are created equally, and it's a matter of public interest if a political figure violates consent or other laws. But if the sex in question is legal and consensual, press reports would be more useful if they included some historical context.

> "Objectivity is a much-misunderstood
> concept and is too often uncritically
> mythologized as central to American
> journalistic practice."

Political Adversity Might Be Strengthening Journalism

Ryan J. Thomas

In the following viewpoint Ryan J. Thomas argues that President Trump's often-expressed mistrust of the media could embolden journalists to become more aggressive. Thomas maintains that Trump's well-publicized feuds with many in the media might prove to be a boon to American journalism. He adds his gratification because he believes a strong and independent media is critical to the well-being of American democracy. Ryan J. Thomas is an assistant professor of journalism studies at the University of Missouri-Columbia.

As you read, consider the following questions:

1. How does the author use historical context to make his points about the present?
2. In what way does the author believe that the dislike President Trump has expressed for the media will strengthen American journalism?
3. Why does the author evoke the name of Cokie Roberts in this article?

"Could Donald Trump Change Journalism for the Better?" by Ryan J. Thomas, The Conversation, April 22, 2016. https://theconversation.com/could-donald-trump-change-journalism-for-the-better-57856. Licensed under CC BY-ND 4.0 International.

It is unsurprising that wherever Donald Trump goes, headlines follow. But what is particularly interesting is just how many of those headlines involve the practice of journalism and journalists themselves.

Trump has called to "open up" libel laws. He has mocked *New York Times'* reporter Serge Kovaleski's disability. He has feuded with Fox News' Megyn Kelly over questions she asked of him during a Republican presidential debate. And then there are the accusations of violence against journalists at Trump rallies.

Trump so challenges the norms and conventions of politics, it has caused some to express anxiety about the "corrosion of democratic culture" as a result of the damage he leaves in his wake.

Journalists, as chroniclers of the political system, are confronted with a dilemma. How should journalists cover Trump's candidacy? Can they—and should they—be objective?

Objectivity is a much misunderstood concept and is too often uncritically mythologized as central to American journalistic practice. What interests me is how the pressure to be objective—and therefore disengaged from the very real impact Trump is having on the democratic process—may impede journalists' crucial role as stewards of democracy.

The Cokie Roberts case

In March, longtime NPR commentator Cokie Roberts received flak from journalists, including some of her NPR colleagues, for coauthoring a column that argued that Trump is

> one of the least qualified candidates ever to make a serious run for the presidency. If he is nominated by a major party—let alone elected—the reputation of the United States would suffer a devastating blow around the world.

Roberts was roundly chastised by her colleagues and NPR executives for failing to adhere to the objectivity norm—this despite her status as a commentator.

Morning Edition host David Greene even expressed his disappointment with Roberts on the air, telling her that "objectivity is so fundamental to what we do" and asking, "can you blame people like me for being a little disappointed to hear you come out and take a personal position on something like this in a campaign?"

Roberts defended her column by describing herself as someone who is nonpartisan but "interested in government working." Her argument was essentially an appeal to basic democratic values and the manner in which Trump is challenging them.

In contrast—and providing a masterful illustration of the tension between journalistic and business values—CBS head Leslie Moonves recently told an audience of investors that while Trump "may not be good for America" he is "damn good for CBS ...The money's rolling in."

Is your analyst my commentator?

NPR's dilemma speaks to broader shifts in the media ecosystem.

A study I coauthored with Elizabeth Blanks Hindman examined the responses of journalists to NPR's decision to fire analyst Juan Williams for comments he made on Fox News in 2010 about feeling "nervous" about sharing a plane with Muslims.

The responses indicated much confusion about Williams' role, with some pondering what exactly it means to be an "analyst" as versus, say, a "reporter" or a "commentator." Others criticized Williams for not adhering to the objectivity norm.

We found similar findings in our study of journalistic responses to the retirement of veteran White House correspondent Helen Thomas following controversial remarks she made that Israel should "get the hell out of Palestine." The majority of responses we analyzed criticized Thomas for failing to be objective regarding the Israel-Palestine conflict, when in fact her role at the time was as an opinion columnist.

We see these findings as markers of broader uncertainties about 21st-century journalism. To question objectivity is to invite the larger question of what we expect of the 21st-century journalist. Is "objectivity," at least as presently understood, fit for purpose?

The fact is that Cokie Roberts is not the only one to express her unease about Trump's candidacy.

The *Huffington Post* has taken to appending an editor's note to every article about Trump informing readers that he is "a serial liar, rampant xenophobe, racist, misogynist, birther, and bully."

The *Boston Globe* attracted attention for a cover that ran on the front of its Sunday edition's Ideas section presented as an account of what life would look like under President Trump, with mass deportations and trade wars the new normal.

How, then, should journalists respond to an authoritarian candidate who incites violence, fuels racial tension and fractures the social fabric by indulging the worst excesses of American bigotry?

"Journalists owe democracy their allegiance"

The first defense of Roberts' column is to point out that it was an opinion column written by a commentator. Roberts was, in effect, doing what she is paid to do: opine. This makes the criticism of her column all the more bizarre.

However, the second and more fundamental defense is to consider at a deeper level how journalists in a liberal democracy respond to phenomena that challenge the very precepts of liberal democracy.

This is a much-needed conversation, and one that has long been stifled by a narrow conception of objectivity. Too often objectivity, as it is practiced, emphasizes neutrality and balance at all costs. This can be seen, for example, in coverage of the human impact on climate change as a question still being debated when an overwhelming majority of scientists believe there is unassailable evidence that it is a fact that needs to be dealt with.

This kind of objectivity positions the journalist as a "morally disengaged" communicator possessing, as the ethicist Ted Glasser argues,

> neither the need nor the opportunity to develop a critical perspective from which to assess the events, the issues, and the personalities he or she is assigned to cover.

In "The Limits of Objective Reporting," the philosopher Raphael Cohen-Almagor argues that

subjectivity is preferable to objectivity when the media cover illiberal and anti-democratic phenomena.

Cohen-Almagor argues—and I concur—that when confronted with issues that challenge the basic values of liberal democracy itself, journalists are called to set aside moral neutrality.

From this perspective, journalism ought to be nonpartisan in party terms but wholly on the side of democracy, good governance and the protection of people's rights and civil liberties.

As Cohen-Almagor says, journalists

live within the democratic realm and owe democracy their allegiance. Free speech and free journalism exist because democracy makes them possible.

This is not so unusual an idea, and ought not be controversial. Indeed, we don't need to go that far back into journalism history to find examples of it.

One of the reasons Edward R. Murrow is regarded as one of the finest American journalists is because of his opposition to the demagoguery of Joseph McCarthy, devoting an episode of "See It Now" to a methodical exposition of McCarthy's smears and deceits.

Murrow recognized the threat that McCarthy (and McCarthyism) posed to the fabric of American democracy and acted with conviction. Where is today's Edward R. Murrow?

Trump is testing the boundaries of the political system. His platform and proclamations, and the manner in which he articulates them, pose such a challenge to regular order that it becomes necessary to ask if the norms of political coverage ought to be rethought.

Perhaps a new journalistic vocabulary is necessary. Trump's candidacy may provide just the occasion for such a rethink.

Periodical and Internet Sources Bibliography

The following articles have been selected to supplement the diverse views presented in this chapter.

Alec Brust, "Brust: Black Lives Matter needs to establish a new means of protest to succeed," The Rocky Mountain Collegian, July 13, 2017.

Carter Eskew, "A Question of Morality in Politics," The Washington Post, May 13, 2014. https://www.washingtonpost.com/blogs/post-partisan/wp/2014/05/13/a-question-of-morality-in-politics/?utm_term=.b59bb008a51a.

"Hillary for America, 'Role models,'" Political Advertising Resource Center. https://parc.umd.edu/2016-ad-analyses/hillary-for-america-role-models/.

George Lakoff, "An Excerpt from Moral Politics: How Liberals and Conservatives Think," University of Chicgo Press. http://www.press.uchicago.edu/Misc/Chicago/467716.html.

Kyra Maquiso, "Do We Really Need 'Morality' in Leadership? (A Close Insight on Moral Leadership)," Carnegie Council's Global Ethics Network, December 30, 2013. http://www.globalethicsnetwork.org/profiles/blogs/do-we-really-need-morality-in-leadership-a-close-insight-on-moral.

Maria Popova, "Lying in Politics: Hannah Arendt on Deception, Self-Deception, and the Psychology of Defactualization," Brain Pickings, June 15, 2016. https://www.brainpickings.org/2016/06/15/lying-in-politics-hannah-arendt/.

Eric Ringham, "Why should the public care about a politician's private life?" Minnesota Public Radio, July 2, 2009. https://blogs.mprnews.org/todays-question/2009/07/why-should-the-public-care-about-a-politicians-private-life/.

Brandon Weber, "Ever heard of 'Black Wall Street?'" The Progressive, February 19, 2016. http://progressive.org/dispatches/ever-heard-black-wall-street/.

OPPOSING
VIEWPOINTS®
SERIES

CHAPTER 4

Are Special Interests Corrupting Politics?

Chapter Preface

E liminating or even limiting the effect of money in politics, both during campaigns and beyond, would be no small chore. Special interest groups pour billions into the coffers of politicians they believe or understand will aid their economic causes. That leads to candidates and those in office sometimes dismissing their values or shedding their beliefs to battle on the side of those providing funds. The result is a weakening of democracy, and constituents often voting for people in all offices that do not truly believe in the issues they for which they are fighting.

Special interests have played a huge role in US politics for centuries. Some are generally distasteful or at least unpopular, including powerful entities such as the tobacco industry or the National Rifle Association. Their influence has led many to call for campaign finance reform or laws that would limit the amount of special interest spending. It is accepted that political debate should be based strictly on the issues and should not be influenced by money. Though that does not technically fall under the category of bribery, politicians married to special interest groups are to a great extent bought and sold.

Most Americans agree that something should be done, but they do not agree on what, and politicians who need money to run campaigns have certainly not stumbled over themselves to create and advance reform. The result is a deepening of distrust among the populace and those they elect to lead them. Opinion polls have proven that Americans generally disprove of the job performance of their senators and congresspeople. Ties to special interests is one of the primary reasons for that unpopularity.

> *"Meanwhile, 85 percent of Americans say we need to either 'completely rebuild' or make 'fundamental changes' to the campaign finance system. Just 13 percent think 'only minor changes are necessary,' less than the 18 percent of Americans who believe they've been in the presence of a ghost."*

In the United States Money Controls Politics

Jon Schwarz

In the following viewpoint Jon Schwarz rather humorously tracks the proclamations of politicians calling for campaign finance reform. Included among them is President Trump, who spoke about what he called a broken system in 2015. Schwarz contends that politicians understand the frustration and anger of their constituents over special interests, so they talk a good game. But few have taken steps to make changes. Among those that did boast about where his money was coming from was 2016 Democratic presidential candidate Bernie Sanders. The result was a level of popularity that many believe should have made Sanders the Democrat's candidate in the general election. Jon Schwarz is a journalist who writes for The Intercept *and has contributed to the* New Yorker, The Atlantic, *the* New York Times, *and other publications.*

"Yes, We're Corrupt": A List of Politicians Admitting That Money Controls Politics," by Jon Schwarz, The Intercept, July 30, 2015. Reprinted by Permission.

As you read, consider the following questions:

1. Which politicians quoted here seem the most sincere in calling for campaign finance reform?
2. Does the viewpoint make any suggestions about what can be done to control special interest groups?
3. How does the author take a tongue-in-cheek approach to presenting the views expressed in the article?

One of the most embarrassing aspects of US politics is politicians who deny that money has any impact on what they do. For instance, Tom Corbett, Pennsylvania's notoriously fracking-friendly former governor, got $1.7 million from oil and gas companies but assured voters that "The contributions don't affect my decisions." If you're trying to get people to vote for you, you can't tell them that what they want doesn't matter.

This pose is also popular with a certain prominent breed of pundits, who love to tell us "Don't Follow the Money" (*New York Times* columnist David Brooks), or "Money does not buy elections" (Freakonomics co-author Stephen Dubner on public radio's Marketplace), or "Money won't buy you votes" (Yale Law School professor Peter H. Schuck in the *Los Angeles Times*).

Meanwhile, 85 percent of Americans say we need to either "completely rebuild" or make "fundamental changes" to the campaign finance system. Just 13 percent think "only minor changes are necessary," less than the 18 percent of Americans who believe they've been in the presence of a ghost.

So we've decided that it would be useful to collect examples of actual politicians acknowledging the glaringly obvious reality. Here's a start; I'm sure there must be many others, so if you have suggestions, please leave them in the comments or email me. I'd also love to speak directly to current or former politicians who have an opinion about it.

"I gave to many people, before this, before two months ago, I was a businessman. I give to everybody. When they call, I give.

And do you know what? When I need something from them two years later, three years later, I call them, they are there for me. And that's a broken system." —*Donald Trump in 2015.*

"[T]his is what's wrong. [Donald Trump] buys and sells politicians of all stripes ... he's used to buying politicians." —*Sen. Rand Paul, R-Ky., in 2015.*

"Now [the United States is] just an oligarchy, with unlimited political bribery being the essence of getting the nominations for president or to elect the president. And the same thing applies to governors and US senators and congressmembers. ... So now we've just seen a complete subversion of our political system as a payoff to major contributors ..." —*Jimmy Carter, former president, in 2015.*

"[T]he millionaire class and the billionaire class increasingly own the political process, and they own the politicians that go to them for money. ... we are moving very, very quickly from a democratic society, one person, one vote, to an oligarchic form of society, where billionaires would be determining who the elected officials of this country are." —*Sen. Bernie Sanders, I-Vt., in 2015. Sanders has also said many similar things, such as "I think many people have the mistaken impression that Congress regulates Wall Street. ... The real truth is that Wall Street regulates the Congress."*

"You have to go where the money is. Now where the money is, there's almost always implicitly some string attached. ... It's awful hard to take a whole lot of money from a group you know has a particular position then you conclude they're wrong [and] vote no." —*Vice President Joe Biden in 2015.*

"[T]oday's whole political game, run by an absurdist's nightmare of moneyed elites, is ridiculous—a game in which corporations are people and money is magically empowered to speak; candidates trek to the corporate suites and secret retreats of the rich, shamelessly selling their political souls."—*Jim Hightower, former Democratic agricultural commissioner of Texas, 2015.*

"People tell me all the time that our politics in Washington are broken and that multimillionaires, billionaires and big corporations are calling all the shots ... it's hard not to agree." —*Russ Feingold, three-term Democratic senator from Wisconsin, in 2015 announcing he's running for the Senate again.*

"Lobbyists and career politicians today make up what I call the Washington Cartel. ... [They] on a daily basis are conspiring against the American people. ... [C]areer politicians' ears and wallets are open to the highest bidder." —*Sen. Ted Cruz, R-Texas, in 2015.*

"I can legally accept gifts from lobbyists unlimited in number and in value ... As you might guess, what results is a corruption of the institution of Missouri government, a corruption driven by big money in politics." —*Missouri State Sen. Rob Schaaf, 2015.*

"When you start to connect the actual access to money, and the access involves law enforcement officials, you have clearly crossed a line. What is going on is shocking, terrible."—*James E. Tierney, former attorney general of Maine, in 2014.*

"Allowing people and corporate interest groups and others to spend an unlimited amount of unidentified money has enabled certain individuals to swing any and all elections, whether they are congressional, federal, local, state ... Unfortunately and rarely are these people having goals which are in line with those of the general public. History well shows that there is a very selfish game that's going on and that our government has largely been put up for sale."—*John Dingell, 29-term Democratic congressman from Michigan, in 2014 just before he retired.*

"When some think tank comes up with the legislation and tells you not to fool with it, why are you even a legislator anymore? You just sit there and take votes and you're kind of a feudal serf for folks with a lot of money." —*Dale Schultz, 32-year Republican state legislator in Wisconsin and former state Senate Majority Leader, in 2013 before retiring rather than face a primary challenger backed by Americans for Prosperity. Several months later Schultz said: "I firmly believe that we are beginning in this*

Does the NRA have blood on its hands after Parkland?

Following last week's the horrific school shooting which left 17 innocent people dead, many have been quick to blame the National Rifle Association (NRA) for fueling the gun addicted sub-culture that played a part in the tragedy. However, a new report shows how the NRA played a more direct role by funding a program that the alleged shooter, Nikolas Cruz, used to help shapen his "marksmanship" skills.

In September 2016, the NRA, as part of their ongoing multimillion-dollar effort to spread the propaganda of their so-called "Second Amendment" gun cult, donated $10,827 in "non-cash assistance" to Marjory Stoneman Douglas High School's Junior Reserve Officers' Training Corps (JROTC) Marksmanship team. The same school Cruz visited on Valentine's day 2018 with an AR-style assault rifle to show his "skills" off to his unsuspecting former classmates.

Cruz, who was expelled from the school for undisclosed "disciplinary reasons," was a decorated member of the JROTC in 2016. Aaron Diener, Cruz's former classmate, and fellow JROTC Marksmanship team member, said that Cruz was very much at home shooting assault rifles.

country to look like a Russian-style oligarchy where a couple of dozen billionaires have basically bought the government."

"I was directly told, 'You want to be chairman of House Administration, you want to continue to be chairman.' They would actually put in writing that you have to raise $150,000. They still do that—Democrats and Republicans. If you want to be on this committee, it can cost you $50,000 or $100,000— ou have to raise that money in most cases." —*Bob Ney, five-term Republican congressman from Ohio and former chairman of the House Administration Committee who pleaded guilty to corruption charges connected to the Jack Abramoff scandal, in 2013.*

"The alliance of money and the interests that it represents, the access that it affords to those who have it at the expense of those who don't, the agenda that it changes or sets by virtue of its power

"He was a very good shot. He had an AR-15 he talked about, and pistols he had shot. ... He would tell us, 'Oh, it was so fun to shoot this rifle' or 'It was so fun to shoot that.' It seemed almost therapeutic to him, the way he spoke about it."

After receiving the NRA's generous "gift," the school's JROTC Marksmanship team was quick to take to Twitter and show their heartfelt appreciation for their benevolent benefactors. In a tweet from September 21, 2016, the team tweeted: "MSD JROTC Marksmanship team would like to thank the NRA for their grateful donation of nearly $10,000 to upgrade and replenish equipment!"

Unfortunately, the school made the team's tweet private shortly after the press tied Cruz to the program.

However, the NRA's website proudly brags about "Investing in the next generation of America's leaders, a significant majority of The NRA Foundation grants support youth shooting sports programs." ThinkProgress notes, "The NRA Foundation operates the Friends of the NRA program, which raises money for youth shooting sports as a way of recruiting young activists to fight gun regulation."

"Blood on Their Hands: NRA Funded $10,000 Towards Training Nikolas Cruz To Be Better Marksman," by Joe Clark, LiberalAmerica.life, February 19, 2018.

is steadily silencing the voice of the vast majority of Americans ... The truth requires that we call the corrosion of money in politics what it is—it is a form of corruption and it muzzles more Americans than it empowers, and it is an imbalance that the world has taught us can only sow the seeds of unrest."—*Secretary of State John Kerry, in 2013 farewell speech to the Senate.*

"American democracy has been hacked. ... The United States Congress ... is now incapable of passing laws without permission from the corporate lobbies and other special interests that control their campaign finances." —*Al Gore, former vice president, in his 2013 book* The Future.

"I think it is because of the corrupt paradigm that has become Washington, D.C., whereby votes continually are bought rather than representatives voting the will of their constituents. ... That's the voice that's been missing at the table in Washington, D.C.—

the people's voice has been missing." —*Michele Bachmann, four-term Republican congresswoman from Minnesota and founder of the House Tea Party Caucus, in 2011.*

"I will begin by stating the sadly obvious: Our electoral system is a mess. Powerful financial interests, free to throw money about with little transparency, have corrupted the basic principles underlying our representative democracy." —*Chris Dodd, five-term Democratic senator from Connecticut, in 2010 farewell speech to the Senate.*

"The banks—hard to believe in a time when we're facing a banking crisis that many of the banks created—are still the most powerful lobby on Capitol Hill. And they frankly own the place."—*Sen. Dick Durbin, D-Ill., in 2009.*

"Across the spectrum, money changed votes. Money certainly drove policy at the White House during the Clinton administration, and I'm sure it has in every other administration too." —*Joe Scarborough, four-term Republican congressman from Florida and now co-host of "Morning Joe," in the 1990s.*

"We are the only people in the world required by law to take large amounts of money from strangers and then act as if it has no effect on our behavior." —*Barney Frank, 16-term Democratic congressman from Massachusetts, in the 1990s.*

"… money plays a much more important role in what is done in Washington than we believe. … [Y]ou've got to cozy up, as an incumbent, to all the special interest groups who can go out and raise money for you from their members, and that kind of a relationship has an influence on the way you're gonna vote. … I think we have to become much more vigilant on seeing the impact of money … I think it's wrong and we've got to change it." —*Mitt Romney, then the Republican candidate running against Ted Kennedy for Senate, in 1994.*

"There is no question in the world that money has control." —*Barry Goldwater, 1964 GOP Presidential nominee, just before retiring from the Senate in 1986.*

"When these political action committees give money, they expect something in return other than good government. ... Poor people don't make political contributions. You might get a different result if there were a poor-PAC up here." —*Bob Dole, former Republican Senate Majority Leader and 1996 GOP Presidential nominee, in 1983.*

"Money is the mother's milk of politics." —*Jesse Unruh, Speaker of the California Assembly in the 1960s and California State Treasurer in the 1970s and 80s.*

"I had a nice talk with Jack Morgan [i.e., banker J.P. Morgan, Jr.] the other day and he seemed more worried about [Assistant Secretary of Agriculture Rexford] Tugwell's speech than about anything else, especially when Tugwell said, 'From now on property rights and financial rights will be subordinated to human rights.' ... The real truth of the matter is, as you and I know, that a financial element in the larger centers has owned the Government ever since the days of Andrew Jackson ... The country is going through a repetition of Jackson's fight with the Bank of the United Stated—only on a far bigger and broader basis." —*Franklin D. Roosevelt in a 1933 letter to Edward M. House.*

"Behind the ostensible government sits enthroned an invisible government, owing no allegiance and acknowledging no responsibility to the people. To destroy this invisible government, to dissolve the unholy alliance between corrupt business and corrupt politics is the first task of the statesmanship of the day." —*1912 platform of the Progressive Party, founded by former president Theodore Roosevelt.*

"There are two things that are important in politics. The first is money and I can't remember what the second one is." —*Mark Hanna, William McKinley's 1896 presidential campaign manager and later senator from Ohio, in 1895.*

> *"More robust disclosure is necessary*
> *so the electorate knows the identities*
> *of those seeking to influence them."*

Candidates Are Increasingly Beholden to Special Interest Groups

Jonathan Backer

In the following viewpoint Jonathan Backer explores Citizens United, a political action committee that funds campaigns for right-wing candidates. Backer perceives such "Super PACs" as dangerous to American democracy by creating an uneven playing field for a variety of candidates. He uses a frequently asked question-and-answer format to explain his points and address his concerns. Backer details how Citizens United works in providing his readers with a warning about the future of the American campaign system. Jonathan Backer is a former research associate for the Brennan Center for Justice.

As you read, consider the following questions:

1. In what way does the author make his views about Citizens United obvious?
2. Does the author provide any answers to the question of campaign finance reform?
3. To what era in American history does the author compare the current campaign system?

"Money in Politics 101: What You Need to Know About Campaign Finance After Citizens United," by Jonathan Backer, The Brennan Center for Justice, September 28, 2012. Reprinted by permission.

Reports on the 2012 election focus as much on the role of big money as they do on the latest polls. One can't read a newspaper without seeing a story on the outsized role of Super PACs or the record-breaking amounts spent by secretive non-profits. Hardly an hour passes on the cable news networks without a report on whether Mitt Romney or Barack Obama has more money in the bank.

While there's no shortage of reporting on the latest fundraising totals, it's a lot harder to find any straightforward explanations of how the current campaign finance system works. To help make sense of the current campaign finance system and how it came to resemble the Wild West, here are some answers to frequently asked questions.

Q: There are a lot of stories about unlimited political spending and million dollar donations. Aren't there limits on the size of political contributions?

A: To understand contribution limits, one has to understand that different limits apply depending on who is giving and who is receiving the contributions.

There are limits on donations to candidates and political parties.[1] The Supreme Court has declared that such restrictions are constitutional because allowing unlimited contributions to elected officials (or political parties) could lead to corruption.[2] Current rules set a $2,500 per-person per-election limit for federal candidates.[3] (Each state sets its own limits on donations to state or local candidates.)[4] There is a $30,800 per-person per-year limit on donations to national party committees, and a $10,000 total limit on per-person contributions to state, district or local party committees.[5]

But different rules apply to non-party, outside groups called political action committees, known as PACs. If a PAC contributes directly to candidates, the most a person can donate to the PAC is $5,000.[6] Significantly, if a PAC declares that it will spend its money totally independently from a candidate's campaign, then there are no limits on donations to the PAC. These groups, which can receive unlimited contributions from individuals, corporations, or unions, are commonly called "Super PACs."

Finally, some non-profit groups, called "social welfare" organizations, or "501(c)(4) groups," can also accept unlimited contributions from individuals, corporations, and unions. The primary purpose of these groups cannot technically be political, but they can spend substantial amounts on political activities, such as TV commercials.[7]

Q: Is there more outside spending this year than in previous years? How much more?

A: Yes. Outside groups are on pace to spend more during this election than ever before. So far, third party groups—including PACs, Super PACs, and 501(c)(4)s—have reported spending nearly $330 million—nearly five times the amount reported at the same point during the 2010 midterm elections and nearly three times the amount reported at the same point during the 2008 elections.[8] With several weeks remaining in the election, the amount of outside spending has surpassed the 2008 total by nearly $30 million, and since outside spending usually spikes in the final month before an election, the total outside expenditures are likely to dramatically increase from four years ago.[9]

Q: About these Super PACs—what are they and where did they come from?

A: Traditional PACs wield influence by either donating directly to candidates or spending independently (by airing television advertisements, for example). But traditional PACS have a contribution limit of $5,000 per-person per-year.

By contrast, there are no limits on Super PAC donations. Super PACs are a consequence of the Supreme Court's ruling in Citizens

United v. FEC. Remember that the Supreme Court previously upheld donor limits for direct contributions to campaigns and party committees because the Court believed that unlimited contributions could lead to corruption. But in Citizens United, the Court declared that independent political spending, because it was not coordinated with candidates, could not lead to corruption concerns.[10]

After Citizens United, a federal appellate court in Washington, D.C. heard a case called SpeechNow.org v. FEC. In SpeechNow, the court interpreted Citizens United to mean that as long as a PAC spends its money independently (i.e. does not contribute to, or coordinate with, a candidate), the PAC is free from any contribution limits.[11] Provided a political committee restricts their spending to independent expenditures, it can accept unlimited contributions. These political committees are what is commonly known as Super PACs.

Q: So Citizens United is responsible for Super PACs. Is Citizens United responsible for the high levels of outside spending this year?

A: At least in part: the extraordinary levels of outside spending this year would not be possible without Citizens United. In the 2010 election, the first campaign cycle after Citizens United, outside groups reported spending $298 million, more than a fourfold increase over the amount of outside spending in 2006, the last midterm election before Citizens United.[12] Prior to 2010, outside groups engaged in political activity were routinely fined by the FEC for accepting contributions that exceeded federal limits.[13] Seven-figure contributions that undoubtedly would have provoked FEC enforcement actions before 2010 are a major source of Super PAC funding today.

As of June 30, 2012, 47 donors contributed $1 million or more to Super PACs, accounting for 57 percent of individual donations to these groups.[14]

If Super PACs had to adhere to the contribution limits in place before Citizens United, they would have raised only $11.2 million in contributions from individuals during the 2012 cycle compared to the $346 million they have actually raised. In other words, 97 percent of contributions to Super PACs would not have been possible without Citizens United.

Q: What about Super PACs that work closely with candidates? How can Super PACs work closely with campaigns if they're supposed to be "independent?" What are the coordination rules?

A: While Super PACs are supposed to be totally independent— after all, that's the only reason they don't have contribution limits— the reality is that they can do a whole lot that looks to most people like "coordination" with campaigns.

The Federal Election Commission sets the rules about what activities are considered independent or "coordinated" with a campaign. At first glance, the rules are simple. As the FEC's website explains, "In general, a payment for a communication is 'coordinated' if it is made in cooperation, consultation or concert with, or at the request or suggestion of, a candidate, a candidate's authorized committee or their agents, or a political party committee or its agents."[15] But the FEC's rules have evolved in such a way that determining what is coordination is now a highly technical and murky exercise.[16]

Unfortunately, the FEC rarely provides clear guidance. Part of the problem is that each party appoints three of the FEC's six commissioners, which makes consensus difficult. A majority vote is required for an advisory opinion. But since Citizens United, the Commission has repeatedly deadlocked on specific questions about coordination and independence. When the commissioners split 3-3, the FEC doesn't issue clear guidance.

In perhaps the most notorious case, American Crossroads, Karl Rove's Super PAC, requested an opinion from the FEC declaring that advertisements were not "coordinated" with campaigns, even if the candidates appeared in the ads and consulted with the Super PAC on developing the scripts. Under any common sense approach, such ads would be deemed coordinated. But not to the FEC—it deadlocked on whether or not such ads constituted "coordinated communications"—and, in the end, the agency offered no guidance at all.[17] In another logic defying ruling, the FEC has said that it is not coordination if a candidate solicits funds for a Super PAC.[18]

With no bright line rules about coordination, and with the FEC allowing conduct that would seem to most people to be coordination, Super PACs can work extremely closely with campaigns without fear of sanctions.

Q: Citizens United also made election spending by corporations legal. How much are corporations spending vs. individuals? What about unions?

A: As of June 30, 2012, businesses had contributed $34.2 million to Super PACs, nearly twice the amount donated by unions ($17.3 million). But individuals dominated giving to Super PACs, contributing more than $230 million.[19]

But the amount of corporate spending cannot be fully determined because of tax-exempt groups that do not disclose their donors. An investigation by the New York Times uncovered several large contributions by corporations to tax-exempt groups, including six- and seven-figure contributions from American Electric Power, Aetna, Prudential Financial, Dow Chemical, Merck, Chevron and MetLife.[20]

By donating to non-profits, corporations can avoid shareholder criticism about using revenues for political purposes as well as consumer reaction to their political stance. Consequently, it is reasonable to suspect that, because of non-profits' ability to hide donations, they are the preferred vehicle for corporate political spending.

Q: Has outside spending benefited one party more than the other?

A: In 2010, conservative groups reported nearly twice the outside spending as liberal groups. So far in the 2012 election cycle, conservative groups have reported three times more spending than liberal groups.[21]

Q: How much outside spending is disclosed vs. not disclosed?

A: During the 2010 election, non-profit "social welfare" organizations—which do not disclose their donors—outspent Super PACS—which do—by a 3-2 margin, accounting for $95 million in spending.[22] Trade organizations such as the US Chamber of Commerce, which spent $33 million during the 2010 elections, are also exempt from federal disclosure requirements.[23]

Initial indications suggest that secret spending by non-profits is playing an equally central role in the 2012 elections. The Campaign Media Analysis Group estimates that as of July 2012, dark money totaling nearly $100 million accounted for two-thirds of all spending by the largest outside spenders.[24] The *Huffington Post* found that groups that do not have to disclose their donors had spent $172 million through the end of July—nearly as much as the $174 million spent by outside groups that do disclose their contributors, though total spending by non-profit groups is likely far greater.[25] ProPublica reports that as of July 2012, two of the largest political non-profits, Crossroads GPS and Americans for Prosperity, have eclipsed the combined ad buys of both Super PACs ($55.7 million) and political parties ($22.5 million) with $60 million in television spending.[26]

Non-profit groups have also dramatically escalated spending on express advocacy—ads urging voters to vote for or against specific candidates. Through September 13, 501(c) organizations have spent $67.4 million on express advocacy compared to $44,000 and $3.3 million at the same point in 2006 and 2008 respectively, the two elections before Citizens United.[27] Though only a fraction of secret outside spending, the figures offer a snapshot of the growing role of undisclosed spending.

Q: How responsible is the FEC for the current system? What about the IRS?

A: The FEC has helped foster today's hidden system of campaign finance. For example, by not clearly defining what constitutes coordination with a campaign, the FEC has opened the door to all sorts of mischief between campaigns and allegedly independent groups, which, unlike campaigns, do not have donor limits. As a result, contribution limits have been rendered virtually meaningless.

The FEC's failure to enforce federal disclosure laws has also enabled large amounts of secretive spending in elections. Federal law requires groups to report their donors to the FEC if they run either of two types of election advertisements: (a) ads that expressly advocate the election or defeat of candidates (e.g., "Vote for Smith");[28] or (b) "electioneering communications" or "sham issue ads"—ads that mention a specific candidate in the days immediately before an election but stop short of saying "vote for" or "vote against" the candidate (e.g., "Call Smith and tell him to lower taxes").[29] But the FEC has issued regulations that open up giant loopholes in federal disclosure law.[30]

The FEC's regulations say that outside groups only have to report their donors if contributions are earmarked for specific advertisements.[31] Unsurprisingly, almost no donors earmark donations in this way, so the FEC's regulations allow outside spending groups to avoid reporting their donors.

The IRS has helped facilitate the current system by not investigating whether non-profits are engaged in extensive political activity and abusing tax regulations. 501(c)(4) organizations are supposed to be "social welfare" organizations, whose primary purpose is advancing the public good, according to the tax code.[32] Yet these organizations are now operating essentially as unregulated political committees. Like the FEC, the IRS has shirked its regulatory mandate, failing to set unambiguous rules about what percentage of funds these non-profits may spend on political activity. The IRS has an obligation to investigate these groups to ensure they're not violating tax laws. The IRS should revoke tax-exempt status for groups that are political committees in disguise and are primarily engaged in election-related activity, but it has not yet done so.[33]

Q: Are publicly-financed elections the cure for big money in politics? Isn't public financing a failed experiment?

A: After Watergate, Congress adopted a public financing system for presidential elections. The system served the country well for more than two decades. Unfortunately, Congress never modernized the system, and the pool of available public funds did not keep pace with the dramatic escalation in campaign costs. As a result, in 2008, President Obama chose not to use public financing for his primary or general election campaigns. In 2012, neither candidate is using public financing.[34] Reps. David Price (D-NC), Chris Van Hollen (D-MD) and Walter Jones (R-NC) have introduced legislation to repair the presidential campaign finance system. [35] A companion bill has been introduced by Sen. Mark Udall (D-CO).[36]

Public financing has succeeded in several states and cities. Arizona, Connecticut, and Maine, for example, have highly successful public financing systems for state elections. In 2011, the Supreme Court ruled unconstitutional one provision of a certain type of public financing that was used in Arizona that provides additional funding to publicly financed candidates facing high-spending opponents or large amounts of independent expenditures. [37] Nevertheless, the Court reaffirmed the basic constitutionality of public campaign financing.[38]

An alternative, New York City's public financing system, has thrived more than 20 years and is a model for national reform.

It poses no constitutional problems. The program is simple, but has powerful consequences. The role of small donors is amplified because donations up to $175 from New York City residents are matched at a rate of 6:1. In other words, a $20 donation is actually worth $140 to the candidate (6 x $20 = $120 + the $20 original contribution = $140). In 2009, small donations and matching funds accounted for 63 percent of the individual contributions in the New York City elections.[39]

Q: What else can be done? What does the future look like?

A: A public financing system based on small donor matching funds can provide an important counterforce to the role of big money. Internet and social media fundraising will make a small donor matching funds system even more powerful. Such a system would decrease the opportunities for corruption of federal officeholders and government decisions. Candidates would have an alternative means to finance their campaigns without becoming obligated to special interests. A small donor matching system should be adopted for both congressional and presidential elections.

But small donor matching funds alone cannot repair the broken campaign finance system. More robust disclosure is necessary so the electorate knows the identities of those seeking to influence them. Congress should pass legislation that replaces the obsolete regulations on "coordination" with meaningful rules that ensure groups claiming to be legally "independent" are not merely campaign subsidiaries. The IRS needs to police groups claiming non-profit status to prevent exclusively political organizations from abusing the tax code by hiding their donors. And the chronically dysfunctional FEC should be replaced by a new agency that does not deadlock along partisan lines, so that the campaign finance laws are actually enforced.

Notes
[1] See Contribution Limits 2011-2012, FEC, http://www.fec.gov/pages/brochures/contriblimits.shtml (last visited Aug. 12, 2012).

[2] Buckley v. Valeo, 424 U.S. 1, 28-29 (1976).

[3] Contribution Limits, supra note 1.

[4] Nat'l Conference of State Legislatures, State Limits on Contributions to Candidates 2011-2012 (2011), available at http://www.ncsl.org/Portals/1/documents/legismgt/Limits_to_Candidates_2011-2012.pdf.

[5] Contribution Limits, supra note 1.

[6] Id.

[7] Alliance for Justice, Election Year Activities for 501(c)(4) Social Welfare Organizations, available at http://www.afj.org/assets/resources/nap/election-year-activities-for-501c4s.pdf.

[8] Ctr. for Responsive Politics, Total Outside Spending by Election Cycle, Excluding Party Committees, OpenSecrets.org, http://www.opensecrets.org/outsidespending/cycle_tots.php?cycle=2012&view=Y&chart=N # viewpt (last visited Sept. 11, 2012).

[9] Spending in October of 2010 accounted for more than 57 percent of the outside spending reported during the election cycle. Calculations based on data from the Ctr. for Responsive Politics.

[10] Citizens United v. FEC, 130 S. Ct. 876, 910-11 (2010).

[11] SpeechNow.org v. FEC, 599 F.3d. 686, 695 (2010).

[12] Total Outside Spending, supra note 8.

[13] Press Release, Fed. Election Comm'n, FEC to Collect $775,000 Civil Penalty From America Coming Together (Aug. 29, 2007), available at http://www.opensecrets.org/outsidespending/cycle_tots.php?cycle=2012&view=A&chart=N# viewpt; Press Release, Fed. Election Comm'n, FEC Collects $630,000 in Penalties From Three 527 Organizations (Dec. 13, 2006), available at http://www.fec.gov/press/press2006/20061213murs.html; Press Release, Fed. Election Comm'n, Club for Growth Agrees to Pay $350,000 Penalty for Failing to Register as a Political Committee (Sept. 5, 2007), available at http://www.fec.gov/press/press2007/20070905cfg.shtml.

[14] Blaire Bowie & Adam Lioz, Demos & U.S. PIRG Educ. Fund, Million-Dollar Megaphones: Super PACs and Unlimited Outside Spending in the 2012 Election 8 (2012), available at http://www.demos.org/sites/default/files/publications/MegaphonesMillionaires-DemosUSPIRG.pdf.

[15] Coordinated Communications and Independent Expenditures, FEC (Feb. 2011), http://www.fec.gov/pages/brochures/indexp.shtml#CC.

[16] 11 C.F.R. § 109.21.

[17] Paul Blumenthal, Karl Rove's 'Fully Coordinated' Super PAC Ads Drive the FEC to Deadlock, Huffington Post (Dec. 1, 2012, 3:59 PM), http://www.huffingtonpost.com/2011/12/01/karl-roves-stephen-colbert-fully-coordinated-super-pac-ads_n_1123999.html.

[18] Peter H. Stone, Democrats and Republicans Alike Are Exploiting New Fundraising Loophole, iWatchNew.org (July 27, 2011, 5:06 PM), http://www.iwatchnews.org/2011/07/27/5409/democrats-and-republicans-alike-are-exploiting-new-fundraising-loophole.

[19] Bowie & Lioz, supra note 14, at 8 fig. 8.

[20] Mike McIntire & Nicholas Confessore, Tax-Exempt Groups Shield Political Gifts of Businesses, N.Y. Times, July 7, 2012, at A1.

[21] Ctr. for Responsive Politics, supra note 8.

[22] Michael Beckel, Secret Donors Underwrite Attack Ads, iWatchNews.org (June 18, 2012, 3:35 PM), http://www.iwatchnews.org/2012/06/18/9147/nonprofits-outspent-super-pacs-2010-trend-may-continue.

[23] McIntire & Confessore, supra note 20.

[24] Id.

[25] Paul Blumenthal, 'Dark Money' Hits $172 Million in 2012 Election, Half of Independent Group Spending, Huffington Post (July 29, 2012, 6:17 PM), http://www .huffingtonpost.com/2012/07/29/dark-money-2012-election_n_1708127.html.

[26] Kim Barker, Two Dark Money Groups Outspending All Super PACs Combined, ProPublica (Aug. 12, 2012, 1:50 PM), http://www.propublica.org/article/two-dark-money-groups-outspending-all-super-pacs-combined.

[27] Robert Maguire, What Citizens United (et al) Wrought: The Shadow Money Explosion, OpenSecrets Blog (Sept. 18, 2102, 12:53 PM), http://www.opensecrets.org/news/2012/09/what-citizens-united-et-al-wroug....

[28] 2 U.SC. § 434(g)(2).

[29] 2 U.S.C. § 434(f).

[30] Josh Israel, Court Rules FEC Ignored Law; Shielded Donors from Disclosure, ThinkProgress (Apr. 9, 2012, 4:00 PM), http://thinkprogress.org/justice/2012/04/09/460378/court-rules-fec-ignored-law-disclosure/.

[31] 11 C.F.R. § 140.20(c)(9).

[32] Social Welfare Organizations, IRS, http://www.irs.gov/Charities-&-Non-Profits/Other-Non-Profits/Social-Welfare-Organizations (last visited Sept. 18, 2012).

[33] Press Release, Campaign Legal Ctr., IRS to Consider Changes to 501(c)(4) Eligibility Rules as Requested by Campaign Legal Center and Democracy 21 (July 23, 2012), available at http://www.campaignlegalcenter.org/index.php?option=com_content&view=article&id=1811:july-%2023-2012-irs-to-consider-changes-to-501c4-eligibility-rules-as-requested-by-campaign-legal-center-and-democracy-21&catid=63:legal-center-press-releases&Itemid=61.

[34] Michael Luo & Jeff Zeleny, Obama, in Shift, Says He'll Reject Public Financing, N.Y. Times, June 20, 2008, at A1.

[35] Presidential Funding Act, H. 414, 112th Cong.

[36] Presidential Funding Act, S. 3312, 112th Cong.

[37] Ariz. Free Enter. Club's Freedom Club PAC v. Bennett, 131 S. Ct. 2806, 2827-2828 (2011).

[38] Id., at 2828.

[39] Michael J. Malbin, Peter W. Brusoe & Brendan Glavin, 11 Election L.J. 3, 15 (2012).

> "Democratic elites, defined broadly,
> shaped the primary before voters ever
> got a chance to weigh in, and the way
> they tried to shape it was by uniting
> behind Clinton early in the hopes of
> avoiding a bruising, raucous race."

Political Parties Might Be Corrupting Politics

Ezra Klein

In the following viewpoint Ezra Klein argues that the 2016 Democratic presidential campaign was controlled by the elites of the party that yearned to see Hillary Clinton battle for the highest office in the land rather than upstart Bernie Sanders. The author believes that this was a tactical error and miscalculation, an opinion that many cite as correct given Clinton's defeat in the general election. Though the author does not claim the nomination was rigged, he does state that the Democratic power base sought to make the Clinton candidacy inevitable. Ezra Klein is founder and editor-at-large of Vox.

"Was the Democratic Primary Rigged?" by Ezra Klein, Vox Media, Inc, November 14, 2017. Reprinted by permission.

As you read, consider the following questions:

1. What facts does the author cite to back his contention that the Democrats wanted Clinton to win the nomination over Sanders?
2. Does the author believe the Democrats miscalculated the chances of Clinton to win the general election?
3. What Democratic officials does the author place specific blame on what she perceived as the ill-fated preference of Clinton over Sanders?

Even for the Democratic Party, the past few weeks have been bizarre. First, Donna Brazile, the former chair of the Democratic National Committee, published excerpts of a forthcoming book in which she says that after she took over the Democratic National Committee, she investigated "whether Hillary Clinton's team had rigged the nomination process" through the DNC, and discovered evidence that they did. "I had found my proof and it broke my heart," she wrote.

In the aftermath of Brazile's bombshell, Sen. Elizabeth Warren was asked if she "agree[d] with the notion that it was rigged?" "Yes," she replied.

Within a few days, both Brazile and Warren walked their statements all the way back. Brazile now says she found "no evidence" the primary was rigged. Warren now says that though there was "some bias" within the DNC, "the overall 2016 primary process was fair."

I have spent much of the past week trying to untangle this story, interviewing people on all sides of the primary and in a variety of positions at the DNC. The core facts are straightforward: As Barack Obama's presidency drew to a close, the DNC was deep in debt. In return for a bailout, DNC Chair Debbie Wasserman Schultz gave Hillary Clinton's campaign more potential control over its operations and hiring decisions than was either ethical or wise. But those operations were mostly irrelevant to the primary and couldn't have been used to rig the process even if anyone had wanted to use them that way; the primary schedule, debate schedule, and rules were set well in advance of these agreements. "I found nothing to say they were gaming the primary system," Brazile told me. And while that contradicts the more sensational language she used in her book, it fits the facts she laid out both in her original piece and since.

But there's a larger context that is more important than what happened at the DNC and is getting lost in the back and forth over joint fundraising agreements and staffing power. The Democratic Party—which is a different and more complex entity than the Democratic National Committee, and which includes elected officials and funders and activists and interest groups who are not expected to be neutral in primaries—really did favor Hillary Clinton from early in the campaign, and really did shape the race in consequential ways.

The irony is that Sanders was a prime beneficiary of this bias, not a victim of it. The losers were potential candidates like Vice President Joe Biden, Sen. Warren, or Colorado Gov. John Hickenlooper—and, thus, Democratic primary voters, who ended up with few choices in 2016. To the extent Democratic primary voters feel like they were denied a broad range of candidates in 2016, and that party officials tried to clear the field to coronate Clinton, well, they're right.

Democratic elites, defined broadly, shaped the primary before voters ever got a chance to weigh in, and the way they tried to shape it was by uniting behind Clinton early in the hopes of avoiding a bruising, raucous race. The question—which is important going forward, not just for relitigating 2016—is whether that was the right decision. I don't think it was.

The 2016 primary really was weird

There were five candidates onstage at the first Democratic primary debate of 2015: Hillary Clinton, Bernie Sanders, Maryland Gov. Martin O'Malley, ex-Democratic Sen. Jim Webb, and ex-Rhode

Island Gov. Lincoln Chafee. Of these candidates, only two—Clinton and O'Malley—were longtime Democrats. For an open primary in an at least plausibly Democratic year, this was an absurdly small field. The Republican primary, by comparison, had 17 candidates competing.

It's easy to imagine Democrats who might have run in 2016. There's Biden and Warren and Hickenlooper, but there was also New York Gov. Andrew Cuomo, Kentucky Gov. Steve Beshear, Massachusetts Gov. Deval Patrick, New York Sen. Kirsten Gillibrand, New Jersey Sen. Cory Booker, and Minnesota Sen. Amy Klobuchar, to name just a few. But all of these candidates, and all the other candidates like them, ultimately passed on the race. Why?

Part of it was that Hillary Clinton seemed almost certain to win the nomination. It's easy to forget now, but Clinton was extremely popular as recently as 2014—Gallup found she was the most popular potential candidate in either party, with a favorability rating of 55 percent. "Clinton's iconic status is, increasingly, the only clear advantage the Democratic Party has," wrote Ross Douthat at the time.

But part of it was the way elected officials, donors, and interest groups coalesced behind Clinton early, making it clear that alternative candidates would struggle to find money and staff and endorsements and media coverage. Clinton had the explicit support of the Clinton wing of the Democratic Party and the implicit support of the Obama wing. She had spent decades building relationships in the party, and she leveraged them all in 2016. "Hillary had a lot of friends, and so did Bill," says Elaine Kamarck, author of *Primary Politics*. This, in reality, is why Biden didn't run: President Obama and his top staffers made quietly clear that they supported Clinton's candidacy, and so she entered the field with the imprimatur that usually only accords to vice presidents.

Political junkies talk about the "invisible primary," which Vox's Andrew Prokop, in an excellent overview, describes as "the attempts by important elements of each major party—mainly elites and interest groups—to anoint a presidential nominee before the voting even begins. ... These insider deliberations take place in private conversations with each other and with the potential candidates, and eventually in public declarations of who they're choosing to endorse, donate to, or work for."

Clinton dominated this invisible primary: She locked up the endorsements, the staff, and the funders early. All the way back in 2013, every female Democratic senator—including Warren—signed a letter urging Clinton to run for president. As FiveThirtyEight's endorsement tracker showed, Clinton even outperformed past vice presidents, like Al Gore, in rolling up party support before the primaries.

The show of strength from Clinton and her allies was a way of warning off other candidates. She had the money, the support, the staff. Did they really just want to run and lose to her—and maybe alienate her and her team in the process?

Most possible Democratic candidates looked at this and decided no, they didn't. They had too much to lose. And so that left a huge opening for a candidate with very little to lose.

How Bernie Sanders benefited from the party's pro-Clinton bias

Just as it's hard to remember what a popular, dominant political force Clinton appeared to be in 2014, it's hard to remember how much more marginal a figure Sanders was. Back then, it was Elizabeth Warren who was thought the champion of the American left, the scourge of the banks, the enemy of the billionaires. Sanders was a gadfly senator with no major legislation to his name who idiosyncratically refused to officially join the Democratic Party. Gallup didn't even include him in its polls.

But freedom is just another word for nothing left to lose. Sanders didn't need anything from the Democratic Party or from Hillary Clinton. He wasn't afraid of her ire or trying to win consideration for a Cabinet position. He wanted his message heard, and the Democratic primary gave him a vehicle to make the world listen.

And then he got a gift. Clinton, in reality, didn't just clear the Democratic field for herself—she cleared it for Sanders also. If he'd been running in a race that included Warren and Biden and Booker, it might have been a lot harder for his voice to break through. But he was really just running against Clinton and O'Malley. He was the only candidate representing the party's populist-liberal wing and, given O'Malley's failure to ignite voters, also the only candidate who offered Clinton's critics a chance to stop her coronation.

Clinton's obvious and overwhelming support among party elites also gave Sanders a potent issue, particularly among Democratic voters who weren't fans of the frontrunner. Sanders's whole message was that the powerful and connected were rigging the systems of wealth and influence against the powerless, and here, in the Democratic Party, was one more example. Look at how few debates there were. Look at the emails in which DNC staffers clearly preferred Clinton. Look at all Clinton's endorsements, her money, her machine. Did this look fair to you? Did this feel fair to you?

"They handed him a wedge issue," says Ray Buckley, chair of the New Hampshire Democratic Party. "It connected to his entire message about the elite versus the people."

Other candidates I spoke to during and after the primaries recalled how hard it was to get money from Democratic funders, how hard it was to attract top Democratic staff. And then there were the Democratic debates—or lack thereof.

"The Republicans began debating every other week beginning in July," recalls O'Malley. "And we were silent until October. Then we had our one primetime debate. That was in Las Vegas. And then we weren't on primetime again until Iowa happened."

It's not clear, in retrospect, that the sparse debate schedule was helpful for Clinton—debates are arguably her best medium. But what's undeniable is that they were a way of limiting the voters' exposure to the candidates.

None of this amounts to a rigging, or even anything particularly unusual. Brazile, for one, notes that she also worked to clear the field when she managed Gore's 2000 campaign. "That's politics," she says. "There's nothing wrong with that."

But it led to a primary in which Democratic voters had few choices, and few opportunities to hear from the choices they did have.

What's a political party for, anyway?

It's easy to bash the DNC's joint fundraising agreement with Clinton, or the leaked emails showing that DNC staffers were supportive of Clinton and frustrated by Sanders. The DNC is meant to be a neutral presence in party primaries, and even minor deviations from that position are affronts.

The harder question in the larger one: What role should party elites play in primaries? It wasn't that long ago, after all, that they fully decided primaries, meeting in smoky back rooms during the political conventions to hash out the next nominee. Before 2016, the reigning political science theory of primaries was called "the party decides," and it argued that political elites still largely decided party primaries, albeit through influencing voters rather than controlling convention delegates.

Today we are unsettled on the role party elites should play. Many Democrats, and many Republicans, lament that GOP elites have completely lost control of their primaries, giving us not only Donald Trump but Judge Roy Moore. As the same time, many Democrats, and the Republican president of the United States, criticize Democrats for retaining too much control over their primaries. (Although Sanders's near defeat of Clinton implies that Democratic elites have less control than is widely thought.)

To political scientists, all of this reads a bit oddly. After all, what are political parties there to do if not influence primaries? "Nominations define parties, so of course party actors are going to fight hard to define it how they want it to be," writes Jonathan Bernstein. "As they should." Still, I think Democrats made a mistake clearing the field in 2016. I even think Clinton's campaign made a mistake clearing the field in 2016. Coronation isn't a good look for anyone, and voters don't like the feeling that someone is trying to make their choice for them. My guess is Clinton would've still won in a larger field, but the win would have felt more earned, more legitimate. And if she lost—if, unlike Sanders, Biden had decided the American people had not yet heard enough about the damn emails, and had run hard on them, and had taken Clinton down—Democrats might have been saved a debacle.

The reason it's unwise for the party to try to decide as firmly and as early as Democrats did in 2016 is the party doesn't have very good information that far before a general election. Candidates who look strong prove weak. Voters who seem satisfied prove restive. Competitive primaries surface unexpected information. If we've learned nothing else, it's that political elites shouldn't be so arrogant as to assume they can predict future elections.

The 2016 Democratic primary wasn't rigged by the DNC, and it certainly wasn't rigged against Sanders. But Democratic elites did try to make Clinton's nomination as inevitable, as preordained, as possible. And the party is still managing the resentment that engendered in voters. "Once somebody doesn't trust you," sighs Buckley, the New Hampshire Democratic chair, "it's very hard to get that trust back."

> "From the data above, I don't think
> you can make a convincing case that
> Sanders cost Clinton the election
> based on how his own voters
> behaved. A higher percentage of his
> voters backed Clinton than her voters
> backed Obama in 2008."

Bernie Sanders Did Not Cost Hillary Clinton the Election

Robert Wheel

In the following viewpoint Robert Wheel examines the effects of Bernie Sanders supporters on the general election after he had lost the nomination during the primary process. The author delves into the oddities of the election year as outsiders such as Sanders and Donald Trump received widespread support while a political insider such as Hillary Clinton lost favor with the voters. He concludes that many factors came into play for Clinton's defeat, including her own poor campaigning, but that abandonment by Sanders supporters was not one of them. Robert Wheel is an attorney and University of Virginia graduate who lives in New York.

"Did Bernie Sanders Cost Hillary Clinton the Presidency?" by Robert Wheel, Guest Columnist, Sabato's Crystal Ball at the University of Virginia Center for Politics, Rector and Visitors of the University of Virginia, October 12, 2017. Reprinted by permission.

As you read, consider the following questions:

1. What major reasons did the author give for his contention that a lack of support from Bernie Sanders did not factor into the general election defeat of Hillary Clinton?
2. Does the author state a belief that the Democrats hurt their own cause during the primary process?
3. How does the author look at how a desire for change from voters affected the 2016 campaign and its results?

After months out of the limelight, Hillary Clinton edged back into view recently with two fits of activity. The first was an announcement that her voters should read Verrit, a website managed by a former Clinton digital strategist that purports to post verified facts for the 65.8 million people who voted for her. One of the site's first such facts was that Bernie Sanders helped put Donald Trump in the White House. Later on, an excerpt from Clinton's new book leaked, in which she blames Sanders for hobbling her in the general election, though she seems far more circumspect about why she lost in general. Still, this all begs the question, did Bernie Sanders really put Donald Trump in the White House?

To answer that question, first we need to acknowledge the limitations of such an inquiry. Individual presidential elections have an n of 1; there's no control group in which there's an election in which Clinton glides through a primary unscathed. Accordingly, one cannot definitively say "but for one event, another outcome would have occurred." Especially one that's so hard to quantify. The Comey Effect can at least be measured to some degree because it occurred when the race was being polled daily, but even then it's impossible to isolate from a universe in which there was no letter sent to Congress by then-FBI Director James Comey just days before the election.

Moreover, Trump's margin was slim, but not so slim that we can attribute myriad exogenous factors to his victory. Al Gore's narrow loss of 537 raw votes in Florida in 2000 can be attributed to any number of small factors (the Supreme Court, Florida voter purges, the butterfly ballot, Katherine Harris, Ralph Nader, his choice of running mate) in addition to the larger issues that plagued his campaign. Clinton's aggregate raw vote loss in Pennsylvania, Wisconsin and Michigan was around 78,000 votes, closer to John Kerry's 119,000 raw vote loss in 2004 (if he had flipped Ohio he would have won) than to Gore's. Accordingly, while there are still numerous events that could have changed the outcome of the election, it's harder to say definitively whether they actually did.

Before we turn to the Sanders effect, we should establish that Clinton was the favorite heading into the general election. In 2008 and 2012 Barack Obama won with potentially durable majorities, and all Clinton really needed to do was get the same voters to back a Democratic candidate for a third time. However, faced with the prospect of a crass and corrupt Republican nominee, she tried to broaden the Democratic electorate as much as possible instead of trying to consolidate Obama's base, ignoring states in the "Blue Wall" like Michigan and Wisconsin and diverting resources to areas she didn't really need to win like Arizona and Georgia. Accordingly, I examine "did Sanders cost her the election" through the prism of whether he cost her votes from the Obama coalition that she was unable to fully replicate.

Next, let's turn to the Sanders effect. It makes sense to look at how his behavior affected (if at all) the following groups:

- Sanders voters who voted for Trump
- Sanders voters who voted for third parties
- Sanders voters who did not vote
- Non-Sanders voters who did not vote for Clinton

Fortunately, the Cooperative Congressional Election Study has collected data that can help guide us in determining whether they would have voted for Clinton if not for the Sanders campaign.

Sanders-Trump voters

The phenomenon of Sanders-Trump voters is perhaps the easiest to dismiss out of hand as costing Clinton the election. Much of the phenomenon is attributable to the function of party registration. Registration with a political party is a lagging indicator. For example, West Virginia was Trump's second-best state in terms of vote percentage and percentage margin (after Wyoming). However, registered Democrats still outnumber registered Republicans in the Mountain State. That's because so many West Virginians registered as Democrats when the state was still solidly blue and never changed their registration to Republican as they started voting differently. Switching party registration involves paperwork and deadlines, so less involved voters don't necessarily get around to making a change. So in closed or semi-closed primary states like Oklahoma, Kentucky, and West Virginia, these ancestral, less-engaged Democrats can't vote in Republican primaries. In 2008, they voted overwhelmingly for Clinton, who was running to the right of eventual-winner Barack Obama. In 2012, these states gave outsized numbers of votes to barely-funded, fringe Democrats running against Obama. And in 2016, Oklahoma and West Virginia thumbed their nose at Clinton and voted for Sanders while Kentucky backed Clinton but by less than a point.

The data bear this out. The Sanders-Trump voters didn't self-identify much as Democrats, had approval ratings for President Obama of 23% (perhaps he'd be a better scapegoat for Clinton among this subset of voters) and were less likely to believe that white people have certain advantages in the United States. This doesn't sound like people who were part of the Obama coalition, nor would they have backed Clinton against Trump in most instances. To be clear, there are some people in this group of voters who might have voted for Clinton if not for the Sanders campaign, but they are the vast minority, and you should be wary of anyone arguing otherwise.

Sanders-third party voters

Of course, Bernie Sanders' voters didn't need to vote for Trump to help out the eventual president. Those who voted for third parties did support Obama a decent amount: 67% of these voters who said they cast a 2012 vote said they voted for Obama in 2012 (though that number probably overstates his support among this cohort—election winners traditionally poll better after their victories) and 59% of all such voters approved of Obama's job performance. But only 10% of these voters called themselves Strong Democrats (25% overall identified as Democrats). Accordingly, while this group was part of the Obama coalition, it was a pretty weak one. Demographically the group was pretty ordinary; close to the national average in gender identity, race, and family income. They were actually slightly less likely to self-identify as liberal than other Sanders voters, suggesting the group is perhaps a bit more contrarian than ideological. In any event, these voters are not the stereotypical "Bernie Bros"—strident, young male liberals who frequently post online. Rather, this is a group that leaned Democratic but was never reliably part of the base. In other words, this group was always going to be the least likely of Sanders' base to stay with Clinton. There's little evidence that he turned these people away from voting for President Obama to voting for President Clinton.

Sanders-nonvoters

Unfortunately we just don't have enough data on the people who voted for Bernie Sanders in the primary but then sat out the general election. When working with such a small sample size it's difficult to extrapolate conclusions about the population. However, I will try to address the behavior of his voters, including those who did not vote, in the following section.

Sanders effect on his own voters

From the data above, I don't think you can make a convincing case that Sanders cost Clinton the election based on how his own voters behaved. A higher percentage of his voters backed Clinton than her voters backed Obama in 2008 or Rubio and Kasich voters backed Trump in 2016. Assuming that his voters cost her the election ignores the fact that, if he had not run, in all likelihood there would have been another credible Democrat that ran against Clinton.

Every non-incumbent presidential nominee has faced a contested primary since Richard Nixon cruised to the Republican nomination in 1960, back in an era where convention delegates were still largely chosen by state parties and not directly by voters. Once voters started electing convention delegates, even sitting vice presidents George H.W. Bush and Al Gore faced competitive primaries. In April 2015, a Gallup poll indicated that Democrats wanted Clinton to be their party's nominee by a 57%-38% margin; that is a strong level of support, but also not one that heralded what might have amounted to nomination-by-proclamation.

More than a third of Democrats, 38%, did not want Clinton to be the nominee, so if Sanders hadn't filled the oppositional role, there would have been some other candidate that did. Maybe Martin O'Malley could have successfully positioned himself as the Clinton alternative. Maybe Elizabeth Warren or Joe Biden would have reconsidered after seeing a weak non-Clinton primary field develop. Maybe one of Sanders' congressional backers like Reps. Tulsi Gabbard of Hawaii or Keith Ellison of Minnesota would have decided to take the plunge, or a liberal celebrity like George Clooney or Mark Cuban would've seen Trump leading Republican primary polls and figure "why not me?"

In any event, it's difficult to tell if another candidate would have done better or worse than Sanders, especially because Sanders could have done better. He got 43% of primary/caucus votes so he outperformed a generic non-Clinton candidate, but not by much. In the 2008 cycle, Obama entered the race in early 2007 when Clinton was also polling well (although her level of support was smaller nationally than it was in 2015), and he managed to win the Democratic nomination.

Moreover, when Sanders said "The American people are sick and tired of hearing about your damn emails" at the first primary debate, he unilaterally disarmed himself of one of the strongest arguments against Clinton: that her (and her husband's) history of dwelling in that gray zone between legality and impropriety made her vulnerable in the general election. Sanders might have won if he hammered home the message that Clinton was unelectable. Based on the CCES data, 36% of her primary voters described themselves as liberal and 9% as very liberal—surely some of them were voting for a candidate that they thought was most likely to win in November than the one they best aligned with politically.

Additionally, Sanders' post-election activities indicate that he is not a very savvy organizer. The candidates that he's endorsed have not performed well and his voter mobilization organization is frequently involved in People's Front of Judea/Judean People's Front squabbling. A more organized candidate might have performed better against Clinton.

Further, Clinton's favorability among Democrats in October/November 2016 was essentially the same as her favorability in April 2015. The numbers were slightly lower, but it'd be difficult to attribute any such drop directly to Sanders considering everything else transpiring between April 2015 and the 2016 general election. And if there was a drop arising out of the primary campaign, it could have been worse if another candidate had been her main adversary.

Accordingly, the idea that Sanders cost Clinton the presidency because of his own voters' behavior simply isn't very compelling. His voters turned out relatively well for her and there's little proof that those who didn't were members of the Obama coalition who would not have voted for Clinton but for Sanders.

Sanders effect on all voters

Of course, there's also the argument that Sanders undermined Clinton among all voters, not just her own. The argument has numerous prongs:

- Sanders' prolonging of the primary campaign past the point he was eliminated diverted resources from Clinton and fueled distrust of her.
- Sanders did not work hard enough to get Clinton elected.
- Sanders' focus on the Democratic National Committee's alleged rigging of the nomination fueled distrust of Clinton.

The first allegation is easy to disprove because it assumes, as do other arguments, that the non-Sanders universe did not have a vigorous primary challenge of Clinton. Sanders admitted that after the April 26 primaries that he was mathematically eliminated (the Democratic Party practice of allowing formally unpledged superdelegates to vote for a nominee makes such determinations inexact) and was only staying in the race to influence the party platform, eventually dropping out and endorsing Clinton two months later, a couple of weeks after she clinched a majority of delegates. This is typical behavior for eliminated candidates:

- In the 2016 Republican primary John Kasich was eliminated in March and Ted Cruz was eliminated on April 19, but both stayed in the race in the hopes of making it to a brokered convention until after Trump clinched the nomination on May 3. In both cases they stayed in the race to deny Trump the nomination rather than affect the platform.
- In the 2012 Republican primary both Ron Paul and Newt Gingrich stayed in the race well after they were mathematically eliminated. Paul was more like Sanders in that the impetus for staying in was to affect the platform, but Gingrich was merely attempting to deny Romney the nomination.
- In the 2008 Democratic primary, Clinton herself was eliminated from winning a majority of pledged delegates sometime in April. However, she stayed in the race through June, endorsing Obama after he clinched the nomination on the last day of the primary season.

So, Sanders behaved exactly as many other eliminated primary challengers, including Clinton herself. Blaming a loss on normal behavior is disingenuous and, in this case, hypocritical.

The second allegation is also easy to disprove. Sanders fully endorsed Clinton at the convention. He campaigned for her regularly and told his supporters not to support third parties. Contrast this behavior to Cruz, who in a primetime convention speech told his supporters to vote their conscience (a rebuke of Trump that led to boos in the convention hall) while Kasich didn't attend the convention, never endorsed Trump, and wrote in John McCain for his vote. Trump has a far better case that Kasich and Cruz let Clinton get too close than Clinton has a case that Sanders cost her the presidency.

The third allegation is more serious than the other two, so it requires a bit of unpacking. In July 2016, WikiLeaks published internal DNC emails disparaging Bernie Sanders and his supporters, asking if there was a way to thwart him in the Kentucky and West Virginia primaries, calling him a liar, and generally being dismissive of his campaign. However, Sanders never walked back his support of Clinton. The blame here really belongs on a) the parties behind the disclosure and b) the inept leadership of the DNC, led by Debbie Wasserman Schultz.

Moreover, Sanders was never going to be the reason people attacked Clinton as crooked. She has been a national figure since the early '90s, and her husband's administration was constantly hounded by investigations and people in and adjacent to it going to jail. Republicans had known for decades that the best way to go after Clinton was by attacking her ethics. And Clinton indulged these critics by engaging in dubious if not illegal behavior like using a private email server and soliciting donations from foreign governments for the Clinton Foundation. Ultimately these decisions were her own, knowing that if she did run for president again she'd be attacked like her husband was, and had nothing to do with Sanders.

So I don't see any compelling reason to think that Sanders somehow cost Clinton the election among people who didn't vote for him. He behaved no different than past defeated candidates for nomination (and was certainly more supportive than the candidates that Trump beat) and refused to turn himself into a victim after the DNC hack.

Conclusion

Turning to the inquiry of this piece, did Bernie Sanders cause Hillary Clinton to lose the presidency? I'm an attorney, so I think the best way to approach some inquiry is to determine whether he was the proximate cause of her loss. That is to say, if not for his candidacy, would she be president?

There are many proximate causes for Clinton's loss, and I think you can divide them into three broad categories:

- The Comey Letter: Perhaps the best validated of any of the causes of her loss, there are numerous proximate causes here: her decision to use a private email server, the Benghazi witch hunt, her husband's visit with Loretta Lynch on the Phoenix airport tarmac, Lynch's failure to stop Comey, Clinton's willingness to keep Huma Abedin as an aide, Abedin's willingness to stay with Anthony Weiner, Weiner's willingness to send sexually-explicit messages to people other than his wife, Comey's decision to send the letter to Congress, and so on.
- Exogenous events: These are harder to prove, but you could make the case for any of these items outside of Clinton's control costing her those 78,000 crucial votes: the media's constant focus on her email server, President Obama's failure to nominate a Supreme Court nominee that'd drive African-American or Latino turnout, people voting for third parties, the Russian disinformation campaign against her, etc.
- The Clinton campaign's own actions: the failure to seriously defend Michigan and Wisconsin, the allocation of resources

to stretch states instead of the Blue Wall, the focus on personal appeal (never high for Clinton) instead of her policy positions (more popular than Trump's), calling half of Trump voters deplorable, focusing on data analytics and voter modeling instead of actually doing the hard work of turning the base out, generally losing a campaign where she was favored and had more resources.

Certainly all of those are more compelling proximate causes than Sanders, but is Sanders himself a proximate cause? Again, I don't think he is unless you assume that Clinton would have had no serious primary opposition. I don't dispute the fact that he did end up costing her some votes. And her 78,000-vote loss was certainly slim enough that it can have multiple proximate causes. I'd be willing to state that Bernie Sanders might have cost Clinton the election if no serious primary challenger emerged in the counterfactual. In Pennsylvania, Clinton would have needed around a quarter of the Sanders voters who didn't vote for her to have changed their votes to win. How many of those people were among the 20% of Democrats who didn't approve of Clinton before Sanders even entered the race? My guess is most of those people weren't going to vote for Clinton anyway, but I doubt we can ever be sure.

If you're a Clinton voter angry at Sanders, is that more compelling than any of the reasons listed above? I don't think so. And if you want Democrats to win back the presidency in 2020, wouldn't it make more sense to dwell on issues that had a bigger impact, and focus on the ones that you can control going forward? I could understand relitigating the 2016 primary if it had caused serious damage, but the fighting appears to be based more on rehashing old grievances than actually winning voters back into the Democratic Party. Frankly, if there's any Democrat other than Clinton deserving of Democratic ire, it's President Obama. It was his neglect of the DNC (he'd been told that Debbie Wasserman Schultz should be ousted as early as 2012) that led to widespread grassroots distrust of the party. It was his naiveté that Republicans would actually consider voting for Merrick Garland that prevented him from nominating an African-American or Latino nominee to the court that could've made the Supreme Court a bigger issue for Democrats. And it was his administration that didn't stop the Comey Letter or publicize Russian interference in the election. If you want to start an intraparty squabble, it's those types of mistakes that the party should seek to avoid repeating.

But your real ire should be directed toward Clinton, who seems to have admitted in her book that ultimately she's the reason that she lost, and her campaign, where some of her staff is still blaming Sanders for their bungling. These people are blaming the media for turning people against their candidate and their primary opponent for not turning out enough voters. You know who else faced media that didn't like him and a party base suspicious of him? Donald Trump! Moreover, what is the point of a campaign other than to improve media coverage of your own candidate and turn out your own voters? At some point they need to take responsibility for their own actions. And if they still think that it was Bernie Sanders' responsibility to turn out enough voters for the Democratic nominee, then they should have done the honorable thing and let him win.

Periodical and Internet Sources Bibliography

The following articles have been selected to supplement the diverse views presented in this chapter.

James Bopp, "Campaign finance reform: The good, the bad and the unconstitutional." The Heritage Foundation, July 19, 1999. https://www.heritage.org/budget-and-spending/report/campaign-finance-reform-the-good-the-bad-and-the-unconstitutional.

Jane Coaston, "After Parkland, gun control is on the table for some conservatives," Vox, February 26, 2018. https://www.vox.com/policy-and-politics/2018/2/26/17042012/parkland-gun-control-conservatives.

Ron Elving, "Repeal the Second Amendment? That's not so simple. Here's what it would take," National Public Radio, March 1, 2018. https://www.npr.org/2018/03/01/589397317/repeal-the-second-amendment-thats-not-so-simple-here-s-what-it-would-take.

Seth Grossman, "Creating competitive and informative campaigns: A comprehensive approach to 'free air time' for political candidates," Yale Law and Policy Review, Volume 22, Issue 2, 2004. https://pdfs.semanticscholar.org/7c43/44558b9d85e874ea5ef33223a08aa5425274.pdf.

Dave Levinthal, "The new Trump: Trying to raise campaign money," The Center for Public Integrity, June 17, 2016. https://www.pri.org/stories/2016-06-17/new-trump-trying-raise-campaign-money.

Mark Schmitt, "3 ways this election could transform money in politics," Vox, October 25, 2014. https://www.vox.com/2014/10/25/7069617/campaign-finance-2014.

"The Solution," Every Voice Center. https://www.everyvoicecenter.org/the-solution/.

"Yes, I'd Lie to You," The Economist, September 10, 2016. https://www.economist.com/briefing/2016/09/10/yes-id-lie-to-you.

For Further Discussion

Chapter 1

1. Should news outlets be regulated to limit openly biased reporting?
2. How have Donald Trump's candidacy and presidency in particular changed news in America?
3. Do you think the American public trusts the media? Provide specific reasons why or why not.

Chapter 2

1. How have Donald Trump and other politicians used the media to their advantage?
2. How has media bias, both conservative and liberal, divided Americans politically?
3. Has the news media in general safeguarded the truth in recent years?

Chapter 3

1. Should presidents back morally corrupt candidates based on political agendas?
2. Is the media doing enough to report lies uttered by politicians?
3. Do politicians have the right to privacy in their personal lives?

Chapter 4

1. Do special interest groups have too much influence on politicians?
2. Should campaign donations from special interest groups be limited?
3. Should the electoral college be scrapped in president elections in favor of a popular vote?

Organizations to Contact

The editors have compiled the following list of organizations concerned with the issues debated in this book. The descriptions are derived from materials provided by the organizations. All have publications or information available for interested readers. The list was compiled on the date of publication of the present volume; the information provided here may change. Be aware that many organizations take several weeks or longer to respond to inquiries, so allow as much time as possible.

American Civil Liberties Union

125 Broad Street 18th Floor, New York, NY 10004

(212) 549-2500

website: www.aclu.org

The ACLU has played a role in every policy debate about campaign finance reform over the years. Although it supports increased openness in campaign funding, it has also opposed important aspects of campaign finance laws through the years in an attempt to protect the speech and privacy rights of those posing no threat of corruption.

Brennan Center for Justice

120 Broadway, 1750, New York, NY 10271

(646) 292-8310

Website: www.brennancenter.org

The Brennan Center has been a leading intellectual and legal force for strong and effective campaign laws. It believes that public financing of elections, strong disclosure laws, and other campaign reforms will reduce the power of money and special interests in our elections. The goal is to return voters to the center of the American democracy.

Campaign Finance Institute

1775 Eye Street NW, Suite 1150, Washington, D.C. 20006
(202) 069-8890
website: http://www.cfinst.org/

This campaign finance policy think tank creates debate in academic journals and has been used by the media and policy makers to gain knowledge on a difficult subject. Its work stimulates further research.

Federal Election Commission

1050 First Street NE, Washington, D.C. 20463
(800) 424-9530
website: www.fec.gov/

This independent government agency regulates, administrates and enforces federal campaign finance law. Its work oversees the financing of campaigns for the House of Representatives, Senate, presidency and vice-presidency.

Independent Voter Project

PO Box 34431, San Diego, CA 92163
(619) 207-4618
website: www.independentvoterproject.org/

The IVP is a non-profit, non-partisan group seeking to better inform voters about important public policy issues and to encouraging non-partisan voters to participate in the electoral process.

League of Women Voters

1730 M Street NW, Suite 1000, Washington, D.C. 20036
(202) 420-1965
website: www.lwv.org

This non-partisan organization seeks a democratic process in which every person has the desire, right, knowledge, and confidence to participate. It believes that women should use their power to create a democracy that is closer to the nation's ideals.

New America

740 15th Street NW, Suite 900, Washington, D.C. 20005
(202) 986-2700
website: https://www.newamerica.org/political-reform/

The political reform program of New America, which began in 2014, looks to launch new strategies and innovations to repair what it perceives as the dysfunction of government, restore citizen trust, and rebuild the promise of American democracy.

Political Media

1750 Tysons Blvd., Suite 1500, McLean, VA 22102
(202) 558-6640
website: http://politicalmedia.com/

The mission of this organization is to clearly and strongly espouse the benefits of the rights and responsibilities of liberty both in the United States and abroad.

Poynter

801 Third Street South, St. Petersburg, FL 33701
(727) 821-9494
website: www.poynter.org/

This self-described global leader in journalism is an instructor and innovator to those who seek to engage and inform citizens in modern democracies. It considers itself a leading resource in the journalism world.

Public Citizen

1600 20th Street NW, Washington, D.C. 20009
(202) 588-1000
website: www.citizen.org

Public Citizen fights for strong campaign finance reform legislation in fighting for the will of the people rather than the influence of moneyed interests. The organization has participated in most of the major Supreme Court cases involving campaign finance issues.

Bibliography of Books

W. Lance Barrett. *News: The Politics of Illusion*. London, England: Pearson, 2011.

Christopher Bartels. *Democracy for Realists: Why Elections Do Not Produce Responsive Government*. Princeton, N.J.: Princeton University Press, 2017.

Bell Books. *Feminism Is for Everybody: Passionate Politics*. London, England: Routledge, 2014.

Hillary Rodham Clinton. *What Happened*. New York: Simon and Schuster, 2017.

James Comey. *A Higher Loyalty: Truth, Lies and Leadership*. New York: Flatiron Books, 2018.

Richard Forgette. *News Grazers: Media, Politics and Trust in an Information Age*. Washington, D.C.: CQ Press, 2018.

Doris A. Graber and Johanna Dunaway. *Mass Media and American Politics*. Washington, D.C.: CQ Press, 2014.

Tim Groseclose. *Left Turn: How Liberal Media Bias Distorts the American Mind*. New York: St. Martin's Griffin, 2012.

Matt Grossmann. *The Not-So-Special Interests: Interest Groups, Public Representation, and American Governance*. Redwood City, CA: Stanford University Press, 2012.

Shanto Iyengar. *Media Politics: A Citizen's Guide*. New York: W. W. Norton & Company, 2015.

Daniel R. Kinder and Nathan P. Kalmoe. *Neither Liberal nor Conservative: Ideological Innocence in the American Public*. Chicago: University of Chicago Press, 2017.

Michael J. Korzi. *Presidential Term Limits in American History: Power, Principle & Politics*. College Station, TX: Texas A&M University Press, 2013.

Robert E. Mutch: *Campaign Finance: What Everyone Needs to Know*. Oxford, England: Oxford University Press, 2016.

Thomas E. Patterson. *Informing the News: The Need for Knowledge-Based Journalism*. New York: Vintage, 2013.

Dan Pfeiffer. *Yes, We (Still) Can: Politics in the Age of Obama, Twitter, and Trump*. Lebanon, IN: Hachette Group, 2018.

Travis N. Ridout. *New Directions in Media and Politics*. London, England: Routledge, 2012.

Michael Wolff. *Fire and Fury: Inside the Trump White House*. New York: Henry Holt & Company, 2018.

Index

S

Sanders, Bernie, 126, 128, 146, 148, 150–151, 152, 153, 154–165
Scarborough, Joe, 132
Schaaf, Rob, 129
Schultz, Dale, 129
Schwarz, Jon, 126–133
Scott, Tim, 98
Seddon, Mark, 83
Seitz, Raymond, 40
sex scandals in politics, 99–112, 113–114, 116–117
Short, Clare, 84
Snoddy, Raymond, 52–53
social media, 12, 13, 55–56, 63, 68, 88
special interest groups and politics, 125, 126–133, 134–143

T

term limits, 14, 29–31, 32, 33
Thomas, Helen, 120
Thomas, Ryan J., 118–122
Thompson, Dennis F., 99–112
Tierney, James E., 129
Toomey, Pat, 98
Trump, Donald, 12, 13–14, 22, 24, 55, 58, 68, 72–73, 78–79, 88, 115, 126, 127–128
and mistrust of media, 118–122
and Roy Moore, 94, 95–98

U

Unruh, Jesse, 133

W

Walker, Steve, 63, 64
Wallace, Mark, 54–55
Warren, Elizabeth, 147
Wheel, Robert, 154–165
Whitford, Ben, 80–85
Williams, Juan, 120
Wright, Tony, 82

Y

Younger, Sam, 84